Starting and Maintaining a Charity in Canada

Adam Aptowitzer LL.B.

Starting and Maintaining a Charity in Canada

NOTICE TO READERS

Laws are constantly changing. Every effort is made to keep this publication and its companion website as current as possible. However, the author, the publisher, and the vendor make neither representation nor warranties regarding the outcome or the use to which the information in this book is put and are not assuming any liability for any claims, losses, or damages arising out of the use of this book or its companion website. The reader should not rely on the author or publisher of this book for any professional advice.

Every attempt has been made to ensure that the information in this book and its companion website are correct at the date of publication. However, all information is subject to change without notice. For current information and advice on your specific circumstances please contact a professional with expertise in the subject matter.

Drache Aptowitzer LLP lawyers can be contacted through www.drache.ca.

Library and Archives Canada Cataloguing in Publication

Aptowitzer, Adam, 1975-, author
Starting and maintaining a charity in Canada / Adam Aptowitzer.

Includes index.
Summary: A comprehensive overview of legal and administrative issues for Canadian charity leaders.

ISBN 978-1-927375-20-4 (pbk.)

1. Nonprofit organizations—Law and legislation—Canada. 2. Nonprofit organizations—Taxation—Law and legislation—Canada. 3. Nonprofit organizations—Canada—Finance. I. Title.
KE1373.A74 2014 346.71'064 C2014-904375-9
KF1388 A67 2014

Starting and Maintaining a Charity in Canada
Published by Civil Sector Press Box 86, Station C, Toronto, Ontario, M6J 3M7 Canada
Telephone: 416-345-9403
www.charityinfo.ca
Publisher: Jim Hilborn
Editor: Lisa MacDonald
Cover Art: John VanDuzer
Interior book design and production: workmark.ca

To my parents, Isaac and Naomi Aptowitzer.
Because (the law of) charity begins at home.

ABOUT THE AUTHOR

Adam Aptowitzer practices in the areas of charity and tax law. He is a member of the bar in both Alberta and Ontario and has been writing and speaking on the topic of charity law for several years. He is a regular contributor to the *Canadian Taxpayer*, *Hilborn Charity eNEWS* and the *Not-for-Profit News,* is often cited as an expert in national media publications and has authored a widely-circulated paper on the regulation of charities in Canada and a second paper on the operation of businesses by charities, both published by the C.D. Howe Institute.

Adam is also a noted speaker and has presented to the C.D. Howe Institute, York University Continuing Legal Education Program, the Legal Education Society of Alberta, the Association of Fundraising Professionals, the Canadian Association of Gift Planners, and the Canadian Bar Association. Adam has given testimony on Parliament Hill and proposed the original idea which became bill C-458. He has appeared before the Tax Court of Canada and the Federal Court of Appeal and will be appearing at the Supreme Court of Canada in the winter of 2014.

In 2012, Adam was named the Heather McArthur Memorial Young Lawyer Award winner by the Ontario Bar Association. He was also named to the "Top 40 under 40" by the *Ottawa Business Journal* and Ottawa Chamber of Commerce and is an executive member of the Canadian Bar Association's Charity and Not-for-Profit Law section as well as the Society of Trust and Estates Practitioners.

TABLE OF CONTENTS

PREFACE

In 1977, I wrote a book dealing with the taxation of charities - the first of its kind (as far as I know) to be published in Canada. That book which had a target audience of lawyers and accountants (the concept of professional fundraisers was in its infancy) was 148 pages and included every Income Tax Act provision, and Revenue Canada (as it was then) document about charities.

Today, the successor to that slim volume encompasses ten loose-leaf volumes and constitutes a comprehensive set of materials for the professional advisor but is not of much use to the average charity volunteer or even a board member.

Thus, the publication of *Starting and Maintaining a Charity in Canada* by my long-time colleague, Adam Aptowitzer, fills a significant need providing a comprehensive overview of the relevant legal issues for those non-experts involved in charities. This audience includes volunteers at all levels and of course directors or trustees.

Aptowitzer is well qualified to write this book as his practice has emphasized the setting up of charities, their ongoing operations and occasionally, their demise. He has a wide experience in dealing with (or occasionally fighting with) the Canada Revenue Agency over issues relating to charities and thus writes from extensive first-hand experience. Also, unlike my original book which limited itself to tax issues, this book ranges far beyond the provisions of the Income Tax Act, covering key federal and provincial corporate issues.

Aptowitzer would be the first to acknowledge that even a complete mastery of this material will not make one an expert. But this book does give one an overview of the astonishing number of issues which a charity's board of directors might face over any given period of time.

In my view, the importance of this book is that it gives those who do not spend day in and day out working in charity law a head's up on issues which he or she may face as a board member, volunteer, or staff person. What is particularly valuable is not only that the arrangement and the writing makes the issues accessible, but that the book allows the reader to formulate the appropriate questions for professional advisers, thereby setting the stage for getting germane answers.

For example, the impact of the GST (or HST in some provinces) is so arcane that even the vast majority of professional advisers are often leery of opining on the issue. But in Chapter 9 Aptowitzer summarizes the rules so that a board member can be alert to situations where a decision may have an impact of GST liability. This prepares the reader to ask an accountant or lawyer specific questions while armed with an overview of the rules.

I would anticipate that this book will become a sort of Bible for those who lead and administer charities and might usefully be given to people who are newly involved with any nonprofit organization as part of an introduction to their duties and obligations.

I highly recommend it.

Arthur B. C. Drache CM, QC

INTRODUCTION

With great privilege comes great regulation.

Historically, many of the responsibilities that are currently performed by government were the responsibility of groups of people – usually religious – who worked to help their neighbour. In modern times these groups of people have become more highly organized and specialized. Governments have learned to work with these groups by sharing responsibility for some areas of charity – such as health care and education – and by creating tax incentives for those who donate to charity.

Unfortunately, with the special privileges accorded charities come great regulation designed to ensure that these privileges are not abused. Such rules are frustrating for the vast majority of people involved in charity who adhere to the principle of helping their neighbour.

This book is written for those people, and for the numerous directors, fundraisers, lay leaders, professionals and volunteers who work for the good of humankind. While there are many rules and regulations that affect charities, just as they affect all actors in society, charities must contend with an extra layer of regulation contained mostly within the *Income Tax Act*. Unfortunately, the Income Tax Act and its various regulations, schedules, interpretation bulletins, guidances and cases are simply inaccessible for the vast majority of charities. And so, *Starting and Maintaining a Charity in Canada* is my attempt to help charities maintain compliance with the law and continue their good work.

While the work in this book is mine, it could not have been completed without the aid of several colleagues. I would like to thank: Arthur Drache for his encouragement in undertaking this project and Alexandra Tzannidakis for her contributions on early drafts of some of the chapters; Eric Brown for his research on Chapter 4 and Jim Hilborn, Lisa MacDonald and Janet Gadeski of Civil Sector Press for bringing the book to fruition.

Finally, the Talmud tells us that the last in the list are those closest to our heart. I want to thank my wife Elana for her constant support in allowing me the time necessary to pursue this project and caring for our daughters Mia and Noa while I researched and wrote. To the extent that this book helps charities heal the sick, feed the hungry, clothe the naked, shelter the homeless, and educate the ignorant it is because of her.

Adam Aptowitzer
Ottawa, Ontario
2014

PART I:

Starting A Charity

HISTORY OF THE LAW OF CHARITY IN CANADA

Canada did not have an income tax until 1917, when funding the First World War made an income tax imperative. At the time, Parliament excluded certain wartime charities from paying tax on their income. In the 1930s, the government of William Lyon McKenzie King proposed changes to the *Income War Tax Act* which would extend tax benefits to charities generally and not just to those named specifically in the original law. The new rules also allowed ordinary Canadian taxpayers to deduct charitable donations from their income. This precipitated the first (and last) serious public discussion about the definition of "charity." Many Parliamentarians felt that to get around the rather intense dispute, the system would simply leave this definition to the courts.

After the passage of the *Income War Tax Act*, it still fell to the provincial courts to review and occasionally update the list of those aims considered charitable. (Of course, now the *provincial* court's decisions also had implications for the *federal* taxability of an organization). Following World War II, the special tax treatment of charitable organizations led to widespread abuses, in particular because of the deductibility of charitable donations from personal income. The abuse was facilitated in part by the fact that any group that held itself to be a charity could accept donations, resulting in special tax treatment for the donor without any real government oversight. As a result of these abuses, Parliament debated a system that would require charities to be registered in order to qualify for special tax treatment. The registration system created a heated political situation when priests of the Catholic Church in Québec felt that their trustworthiness as clergy was being impugned. In their opinion, there was no reason to license any particular type of church organization.

Despite the political firestorm, the *Income Tax Act* was amended again in the 1960's to require charitable organizations to be registered in order to receive the twin benefits of tax-exempt income for themselves and tax-"deductible" donations for their donors. The registration system went live in 1967 with a total of 13,000 registered charities. Future inclusion in the registry was left to the newly-formed Charities Directorate of Revenue Canada (as the Canada Revenue Agency was then known). This task required the Directorate to apply the common law definition of charity to candidates for registration.

Upon Confederation, the power to determine what was, or was not, charitable fell exclusively to the Provincial Courts, a situation that still exists today. However, disputes over registration under the *Income Tax Act* (once the registration system was implemented) did not go to Provincial Courts, but rather went straight from Revenue Canada to the Federal Court of Appeal. So while, technically, the Federal Court of Appeal does not have any jurisdiction to define what is or is not a charity, it does have authority to define what is or is not eligible for registration. Because this includes determining what is charitable, the Federal Court of Appeal became the predominant court for resolving issues of charitable aims in Canada.

Predictably, the convoluted history of charity law in Canada has led to a convoluted situation for charities in operation today. As it stands, for a charity to achieve registration it must comply with the CRA's understanding of the definition of "charity," which is not necessarily the same as a given provincial definition, and it must also comply with any additional restrictions placed upon a charity by the *Income Tax Act*. If a dispute arises as to whether it is eligible for registration, it must appeal any decision of the CRA to the Federal Court of Appeal.

To further complicate the issue, some other areas affecting charities are exclusively provincial. For example, when dealing with legislation regarding fundraising or property taxes, a charity must comply with provincial understandings of what qualifies as "charitable."

Navigating the maze of charity law in Canada can be extremely difficult, and professional advice is required to ensure that all perspectives on an issue have been considered.

WHAT CAN BE DONATED?

Anything can be freely given to a charity, be it money, gifts (such as clothing), or services (such as volunteer time.) However, while the *Income Tax Act* allows receipts to be issued for property, no receipts may be issued for the donation of services. The legal definition of property can be somewhat tedious, but essentially it grants the owner rights over some definable item. This is perhaps an obvious description when discussing something tangible such as land, a car, gold or a table, but it becomes more difficult when discussing intangibles such as corporate shares or patents.

A service is effectively anything that is not property. Again, certain concepts are obvious. One would certainly expect a volunteer at a bake sale to be volunteering a service. However, the definition extends to professionals who offer their services to the charity. A lawyer, plumber, accountant, or painter who provides their professional services to the charity cannot receive a receipt for the value of those services, even though they would normally have received payment.

WHAT IS A GIFT?

In law, there are three elements that must occur for a gift to be valid:

1. There must be delivery of a piece of property. This requires i) something to be delivered, and ii) a sufficient act of delivery.

a. From a legal perspective, "property" implies either a tangible piece of property (such as furniture, a watch, or books) or the bundle of rights that allows control over an intangible piece of property (such as corporate shares, or intellectual property). In order to meet this test, the property that makes up the gift must be clear.

b. There must be transference of ownership. This implies that the ownership of the item was clear and that its control was effectively transferred, both legally and practically. In some cases this is fairly easy to establish. For example, transference of ownership of a watch is clear. On the other hand, transference of some other items relies on the completion of documents transferring ownership. For example, shares of publicly-traded corporations require the completion of legal documentation to transfer the shares from the name of one owner into the name of another. Finally, some objects have ownership transferred by way of constructive transfer, such as a car having legal ownership effected with legal documents but being practically transferred by simply handing over the keys.

2. There must be the intention to give. This is usually clear from the transaction, but the most important element of this test is that there is no payment (in either money or barter) for the item being transferred.[1]

3. Finally, there must be acceptance of the gift. While this is often glossed over by most charities and assumed by most donors, the recipient of a gift can in fact refuse to accept it. This sometimes happens when a charity receives a gift from a politically unpalatable donor. In one famous example, Bette Midler donated a large sum of money to her alma mater, a religious girls' school, but the school refused the gift because it disapproved of the way she was living her life.

TAX FUNDAMENTALS

The *Income Tax Act* is an immensely complicated document comprising sections, subsections, paragraphs, subparagraphs, clauses and sub-clauses in thousands of pages, with cases and commentaries to help explain the law. Part of the reason for the complexity of the Act is that the government uses it to encourage certain behaviours and discourage others. Donating to charity is one of the behaviours the Act encourages. In order to understand how donations are encouraged one must first understand the basic structure of the Act.

1 While this is the technical requirement, the current law does allow for partial payment for a gift with the part not paid for being considered a gift and therefore receiptable.

Income vs. Capital

When a gift is made to a charity, the taxes payable by the donor are not technically the charity's concern. Practically speaking, however, charities can hardly encourage donations when they do not understand the actual cost of those donations to the donors. In fact, charities that truly understand the cost of the donation can be more successful in raising funds - especially large donations. A successful charity understands that the taxes owing on donated items are a major practical concern.

Not surprisingly, the Income Tax Act taxes income. However, the term "income" is not a completely straightforward description of what it is actually taxed. For most individuals it includes salary, pensions, business earnings and other cash accumulated during the year. There are various rules for calculating the percentage of these earnings included in income for tax purposes. However, taxable income can also include the net amount of any gains from the "disposition" (i.e. the sale, giving away, or otherwise loss of ownership) of capital items. Effectively, a capital item is anything that produces revenue. For example, to a taxi driver that owns just one car the car is a capital property, but to a car salesman that same car is inventory. Cars are just one example – in truth, just about any property can qualify as either capital property or inventory, including intellectual property and shares of a corporation. Unfortunately, the distinction is subjective and heavily dependent on the type of property and the use the owner makes of it.

In Canada, capital taxes are levied on the gain in value on the property during the time it was owned by the person disposing of it. When property loses value, no tax is paid. The law contains a variety of rules for calculating gain, depending on the type of property and the tax consequences that arise on the disposition of that property. The disposition of a capital item results in a capital gain if the property has increased in value during the period of ownership, taking into account any costs that went into owning the capital item. Under the Income Tax Act, only 50% of the gain is included in income for tax purposes. So, one is better off earning wealth through capital gains rather than through salary (for example).

Donations

In the context of charitable donations, when cash earned in a year is donated to charity it is nevertheless included in income for the year. If a capital good is donated to charity, the proceeds of the disposition are generally included in income, pending any special tax treatment in the Act. The donation tax credit or deduction is then applied later in the process. This is described in more detail in Chapter 3.

For the most part, it may be impossible for a charity to know whether a particular item is being held as a capital item or as inventory by a particular donor, as this may not be obvious. However, charities should be aware that the consequences to the donor depend on how the property is held.

Deductions

Once all the income is added up, the Income Tax Act allows for certain deductions from income which are not considered taxable. The big one for most people is the RRSP deduction. Ignoring other deductions and the basic personal exemption - if someone earned $100,000 and transferred $10,000 to their RRSP, only $90,000 of their income would be taxable. Charitable donations by corporations (not individuals) are also treated as deductions from income.

Once the net income (i.e. total income minus deductions) is determined, the various tax rates and brackets are applied. The federal formula and most provincial and territorial formulas tax progressively. This means that the first bracket is taxed at a lower rate than the next bracket, and so on. Below is an example using the 2014 federal rates:

- 15% on the first $43,953 of taxable income
- 22% on the next $43,954 of taxable income (on the portion of taxable income over $43,953 up to $87,907)
- 26% on the next $48,363 of taxable income (on the portion of taxable income over $87,907 up to $136,270)
- 29% of taxable income over $136,270

The same calculation that takes place federally also takes place provincially, although there may be a few extra deductions and the rates and brackets for the provinces are different than that for the federal government and from each other. A list of the various tax rates and brackets as of January 1, 2014 follows:

Table of Provincial / Territorial Tax Rates[2]

Provinces/territories	Rate(s)
Newfoundland and Labrador	7.7% on the first $34,254 of taxable income, + 12.5% on the next $34,254, + 13.3% on the amount over $68,508
Prince Edward Island	9.8% on the first $31,984 of taxable income, + 13.8% on the next $31,985, + 16.7% on the amount over $63,969
Nova Scotia	8.79% on the first $29,590 of taxable income, + 14.95% on the next $29,590, + 16.67% on the next $33,820, + 17.5% on the next $57,000, + 21% on the amount over $150,000

2 Taken from http://www.cra-arc.gc.ca/tx/ndvdls/fq/txrts-eng.html

Provinces/territories	Rate(s)
New Brunswick	9.68% on the first $39,305 of taxable income, + 14.82% on the next $39,304, + 16.52% on the next $49,193, + 17.84% on the amount over $127,802
Quebec	Go to **Income tax rates** (Revenu Québec Web site).
Ontario	5.05% on the first $40,120 of taxable income, + 9.15% on the next $40,122, + 11.16% on the next $433,848, + 13.16 % on the amount over $514,090
Manitoba	10.8% on the first $31,000 of taxable income, + 12.75% on the next $36,000, + 17.4% on the amount over $67,000
Saskatchewan	11% on the first $43,292 of taxable income, + 13% on the next $80,400, + 15% on the amount over $123,692
Alberta	10% of taxable income
British Columbia	5.06% on the first $37,606 of taxable income, + 7.7% on the next $37,607, + 10.5% on the next $11,141, + 12.29% on the next $18,504, + 14.7% on the next $45,142, + 16.8% on the amount over $150,000
Yukon	7.04% on the first $43,953 of taxable income, + 9.68% on the next $43,954, + 11.44% on the next $48,363, + 12.76% on the amount over $136,270
Northwest Territories	5.9% on the first $39,808 of taxable income, + 8.6% on the next $39,810, + 12.2% on the next $49,823, + 14.05% on the amount over $129,441
Nunavut	4% on the first $41,909 of taxable income, + 7% on the next $41,909, + 9% on the next $52,452, + 11.5% on the amount over $136,270

Credits

Once the taxpayer knows the gross amount of tax *payable* for a year, he or she can deduct any applicable tax credits. In other words, a tax credit directly reduces the amount payable, whereas a tax deduction simply reduces the amount of income upon which tax was calculated. Donations to charity by individuals result in tax credits. For example, if a taxpayer owes $10 in tax but is entitled to tax credits of $9, she will only be liable for a tax of $1.Thus, they can be very valuable to a donor who has tax owing to the government. (Donations by corporations are tax deductions.)

The calculation of tax credits resulting from donations is fairly simple. The federal government applies the lowest tax credit rate (i.e. 15%) on the first $200 of value donated and the highest rate (29%) on all amounts in excess of that. All the common law provinces except Alberta and Ontario follow a similar system, applying the provincial tax rates at their highest and lowest rates on the level of donation. Alberta gives a tax credit of 10% on amounts below $200, and 21% on anything beyond and Ontario matches the highest rate up to the $500,000 bracket only. The result is that for most people, unless you are already being taxed in the highest bracket, the donation tax credit more than offsets the tax on a dollar donated, and at the highest bracket (except in Alberta and Ontario) the offset is exactly equal. In Alberta the offset is always higher than the tax the donor would have paid on the dollar donated. Ontario and British Columbia apply the second highest provincial rate.

Many people think that donating a dollar to charity is donating a dollar that they otherwise would have paid in tax. “Better it should go to charity than the government” is a common refrain, but the truth is that any donation still requires some pain on the part of the donor. In British Colombia, for example, at the highest possible combined tax rates a donor would pay about 46 cents in tax on a dollar earned, and would keep 54 cents. If that taxpayer decided to donate that dollar to charity he would basically be donating 54 cents, with the government(s) contributing the other 46 cents. The donor is still out 54 cents for every dollar donated.

Donations by corporations

Corporations can donate the same “things” as individuals, but their tax treatment differs. Donations by corporations do not generate tax credits, just deductions. The difference, as described above, is that a deduction reduces *only* the taxable income upon which tax is calculated, whereas a credit actually reduces the amount of tax payable. Given the choice, a donor would always prefer to receive a credit as opposed to a deduction.

Corporate donations to charity that also serve a business purpose can be deducted regardless of whether a charitable donation tax receipt has been issued. For example, a corporation that makes X-Ray machines may justify donating cash to the hospital for the business purpose of maintaining the hospital's good will. Determining whether the donation (or what percentage of it) qualifies as a business expense can be difficult. Ultimately though, it is in the corporation's best interests to have the charitable donation tax receipt; because if the CRA disagrees that the "donation" serves a business purpose, the corporation can always rely on the fact that it was deductible by virtue of being a charitable donation. Nevertheless, the charity would still be responsible for deducting from the amount of the receipt the total value of goods or services returned to the donor or to people not at arm's length from the donors.

Donations by individuals

The federal government collects taxes on its own behalf and personal taxes on behalf of all the provinces except Québec. In almost all of these jurisdictions, the governments provide tax credits equal to the lowest marginal rate on the first $200 of donations and at the highest rate on all donations after the first $200. Because our system levies income taxes based on increasing rates (except in Alberta), the after-tax cost of donating more than $200 increases as overall income increases. For example, if the donors in the highest bracket donate amounts greater than $200, it will offset the taxes otherwise owing. The exception to this rule is Alberta, which provides tax credits for donations in excess of even the highest marginal rates. Thus, in all cases, the provincial government effectively subsidizes the donation.

The tax rates are applied to the aggregate amount of the donor's receipts in a year. Thus, the rules above apply regardless of the item donated. At the end of this chapter a chart demonstrates the relative credits associated with a $1,200 donation. This should not be confused with the after tax cost of donating a capital item, a calculation that requires several additional factors to be taken into account.

First Time Donor's Credit

As the name would imply, the First Time Donor's Credit is designed as an incentive to encourage first time donors to give to charity. It also applies to those who have not used a receipt in the previous five years. Fundamentally, it increases the federal rate of the credit by 25% up to $1000. This would equal 40% on the first $200 and 54% on the next $800.

The enhanced credit is only available in the first year a donor or spouse (including common law) claim it and if claimed for say $20, the credit is no longer available for the remaining $980. On the other hand, the donor does not need to necessarily claim the credits in any of the years and could collect all of the donations to claim one larger credit in the fifth year after making the first donation. The credit expires in 2017.

Limits on donations

It may surprise many Canadians to know that the Act places limits on the amount of income for which a donor can use a tax credit (or deduction) in a particular year. This amount is limited to 75% of the taxable income of the donor in a particular year, subject to certain exclusions. This limit does not apply to a donation made by will in the year of death, where a bequest by Will could not only offset 100% of the tax owing in the year of death but could be carried back to offset up to 100% of the tax owing in the previous year. There are certain other elements of making a donation in the year of death which are discussed in Chapter 5.

Carry-forwards

A tax credit can be used to offset tax owing in the year of the donation and any of the next five years. A donation of $1000 in 2014 can offset taxes in 2014, 2015, 2016, 2017 or 2018, until the credit is depleted. Donation tax credits cannot be carried back to offset tax in a previous year (except in the case of a gift by Will).

Gifts by Will

One legal requirement of a gift is actual delivery of the gift to the recipient. However, where a gift is made by Will, such delivery is impossible until after the death of the person – sometimes well after. Under normal circumstances, the gift would not be complete until delivery is made. However, the law allows that where a gift is made by Will, it will be considered to have been made by the deceased in the few seconds preceding death, assuming of course that delivery occurs at some point after the death. In this way, the tax credits that are generated by the donation can be applied to the donor's year of death. This is particularly useful, as there is often a large tax bill owing on death.

The CRA does allow, by administrative policy (which can change at any time), certain ambiguities in the certainty of the recipient and the amount of the gift. This means the donor does not necessarily need to decide at the time of writing the Will which charity will receive the gift. Specifically, the CRA will allow the executor of the Will to pick a charity from a list in the Will. Of course, only the charity or charities receiving a gift may issue a tax receipt. The other ambiguity allowed by the CRA is when the taxpayer does not specify the amount that a charity is going to get, but rather allows for the division of certain assets or the residue of a Will to go to charity.

The Act also allows for certain differen[illegible]spec-tive. As previously discussed, a donor is ge[illegible]5% of their taxable income using donation tax [illegible]er, in the year of death (i.e. from January 1st u[illegible]h) the donor is entitled to offset up to 100% of [illegible] execu-tor. Any unused donation tax credits ca[illegible]e year preceding death, and be used to offset 1[illegible]at year as well. Obviously, if the return for the [illegible]dy been filed, then it will be necessary to file a[illegible]o claim the donation tax credits.

Provincial residency

As usual in tax matters, the various provinces add an additional layer of complexity to the calculation of taxes and, by extension, donation tax credits. Most provinces follow the same general pattern as the federal government. That is, donation tax credits on the first $200 of the donation are calculated based on the lowest tax rate of the province. Donations over and above the first $200 are given tax credits at the highest marginal tax rate of the province. Alberta calculates this top tax rate at 50% even though its highest tax rate is a combined 39%.

Below is a chart of the lowest and highest tax rates for the various provinces. The donation tax credit is calculated the same way for both the federal and provincial governments. The lesser of $200 or the amount of the donation is multiplied by the lowest tax rate in both the federal system and that of the donor's province of residence. If more than $200 was donated in a year, the calculation is $200 x (the combined lowest federal and provincial rates), + (the rest of the donation) x (the combined highest federal and provincial rates).[3]

The following table provides examples of the differences residency makes to the calculation of the gross tax amount.

Province	Tax Credit Rate on first $200 donation	Tax Credit	Tax Credit Rate on next $1000 of donations	Tax Credit on next $1000 donation	Total combined Federal and Provincial Tax Credit
Alberta[1]	25.00%	$ 50.00	50.00%	$500.00	$ 550.00
British Columbia	20.06%	$ 40.12	43.70%	$437.00	$ 477.12
Manitoba	25.8%	$ 51.60	46.40%	$464.00	$ 515.60

3 Except in those provinces which apply the second highest - Ontario and British Columbia.

Province	Tax Credit Rate on first $200 donation	Tax Credit	Tax Credit Rate on next $1000 of donations	Tax Credit on next $1000 donation	Total combined Federal and Provincial Tax Credit
New Brunswick	24.68%	$ 49.36	46.84%	$468.40	$ 517.76
Newfoundland	22.70%	$ 45.40	42.30%	$423.00	$ 468.40
Northwest Territories	20.90%	$ 41.80	43.05%	$430.50	$ 472.30
Nova Scotia	23.79%	$ 47.58	50.00%	$500.00	$ 547.58
Nunavut	19.00%	$ 38.00	40.50%	$405.00	$ 443.00
Ontario[2]	20.05%	$ 40.10	40.16%	$401.60	$ 441.70
Prince Edward Island[3]	24.80%	$ 49.60	45.70%	$457.00	$ 506.60
Saskatchewan	26.00%	$ 52.00	44.00%	$440.00	$ 492.00
Yukon	22.04%	$ 44.08	41.76%	$417.60	$ 461.68

1 The tax credit for donations over $200 more than offsets the taxes that would otherwise have been due.

2 When the provincial surtaxes are taken into account, the offset at the highest marginal rates is 46%.

3 As PEI charges surtaxes when provincial tax exceeds $12,500, the effect of the offset is higher with income over approximately $98,000 (assuming a single individual with only the basic personal exemption).

2

Charity Structure

The use of the term "charity registration" is well-known in Canada but few have ever stopped to think about what this means. Fundamentally, it means that in order to be registered as a charity, an entity must first exist that is capable of registration. In the same way a baby must be born before its birth can be registered so too must the charity be created before it can become a *registered* charity.

This also implies that a charity can be created that is not registered as such. While these are relatively rare in Canada because unregistered charities do not get the same tax benefit as registered ones, it is technically possible. However, because most people intending to do good works do require the benefits of registration with the Canada Revenue Agency this book deals with the rules for obtaining and keeping *registered* charity status.

It is important to remember that the process by which an organization is created and the process by which it becomes registered are different and carried out through separate means. Registration as a charity is *only* carried out by the CRA while organizing *never* involves the CRA. There are several different forms under which an organization can be constituted, and incorporation can be accomplished either federally or provincially. This chapter will review the different forms of organization and outline some of the ongoing maintenance responsibilities that the different forms of organizations require.

UNINCORPORATED ASSOCIATION

The first and most basic way an association can be organized is simply as a group of people that get together to do good work. Typically this involves friends or neighbors who identify a need and seek to address it through common action.

The rules by which such an organization may operate are entirely up to the group (so long as they do not contravene any laws). For example, they may involve everybody having a similar say in the running of the organization or it may be structured as a hierarchy. Voting can take place as the group decides, or not at all, and there may or may not be any terms for termination of membership in the group.

In order to obtain registration as a charity the group will have to produce some form of constituting document. This could have a variety of different names. It could be called a constitution, memorandum of association, or have some sort of religious nomenclature. What they all have in common are a name for the group, charitable objects, and a dissolution clause. The dissolution clause is critical for the CRA to register the organization as a charity. Typically it requires that on dissolution, the assets of the charity are distributed to qualified donees as that term is defined under the Income Tax Act. Organizations may also wish to include an amending clause in the constitution should they encounter any reason to amend the documents in the future. A sample constitution is available at **www.runningacharity.ca**.

While organizing as an association has its advantages, for example being easy and inexpensive, there are also certain disadvantages. First among them is the general lack of liability protection for the members of the group. That is to say that liability for unpaid bills or damages which may be caused in the course of the charity's operations become the personal obligations of the members. This is also true of legal obligations such as source deductions from employees. In fact, if the organization is ever revoked, the members of the group could become personally responsible for the revocation tax (under certain circumstances). Even though nobody plans to owe money to the government (or anyone else) we generally advise not to operate as an unincorporated association because of the difficult personal consequences which may arise if the charity does run into financial difficulties.

One other disadvantage is the inherent lack of formality within an unincorporated group. The lack of bylaws and the lack of statute to govern the actions of such an operation may be seen as a plus, but in fact members of the group often do not know how to properly operate the group in the event that certain circumstances arise (such as termination of membership or a dispute over control of the organization). Consequently, if a difficult situation arises the organization may become ungovernable.

Unincorporated associations are also limited in other ways. For example, a private foundation cannot be set up as an unincorporated association. Furthermore, an unincorporated group cannot guarantee a loan or own real estate in its own name (with certain exceptions for religious organizations).

In circumstances where the charity knows for certain it will not be engaged in any type of actual operation and exists solely to dispense funds to other charities; there may be some sense in using an unincorporated association. However, in the long run, and certainly for groups that propose to carry on actual fundraising operations and pursue charitable objects, an unincorporated association has inherent risks which can easily be avoided by pursuing incorporation as discussed below.

CHARITABLE TRUST

The Statute of Elizabeth was necessary because at the time, charitable trusts were created when an individual would, by Will, leave their assets for particular uses. In return, the state would accord them special treatment. A trust is effectively a relationship between people governing the use of property. A typical trust defines who would legally own property and who would have the rights to benefit from that property. A charitable trust is one which divides legal ownership over the property from the objects for which that property may be used. This is the reason why we describe the reasons for which a charity exists as charitable objects or purposes.

To this day, a registered charity can be set up as a charitable trust. Typically this involves a trust deed (i.e. document) which explicitly describes the operation of the trust from a governance perspective and which also includes the charitable objects and the dissolution clause. The operation of a trust is somewhat more formal than that for an unincorporated association as there are standard ways in which a trust operates. They therefore retain much of the flexibility that is inherent with an unincorporated association but have somewhat more guidance in certain circumstances.

Again, similar to the unincorporated associations, the liabilities of the trust become the liabilities of the trustees of the trust automatically. It is for this reason that there is often little practical reason to prefer a trust over an unincorporated association. Nevertheless, a trust may be useful where the statute to which a corporate entity (see below) would be subject contains undesirable elements (such as requiring an audit). If an organization wanted to avoid organizing as a corporation subject to those rules and at the same time retain some level of formality in its operations it may opt to organize as a trust.

Organizing as a trust may be a consideration in the same circumstances where one may consider using an unincorporated association. Namely where the entity will exist solely to disburse funds rather than carry out charitable operations. Because a private foundation can be organized as a charitable trust but not an unincorporated association, families may consider setting up a trust for the dispersal of funds. In all other respects, a charitable trust that wishes to qualify for registration as a charity must comply with the same income tax rules that apply to every other registered charity. And like unincorporated associations, trustees may find that the tax obligations for employees or even the revocation tax may become the personal liabilities of the trustees should the organization run into trouble. A sample trust deed can be found on the website for this book at **www.runningacharity.ca**.

CORPORATIONS

The use of a corporation to organize as a charity is by far the most popular option. One reason may be that many people are familiar with corporations in a private company context involving shares, directors and officers. Corporations that operate charities (typically called charitable corporations) are, in fact, corporations without share capital. This means that instead of shareholders there are members. The members elect the directors and depending on the bylaws, the officers of the corporation may be elected by the members or appointed by the directors.

Typically the members of the corporation are admitted by the directors and the directors are elected by the members. The way out of this "chicken and egg" problem is that in some jurisdictions the original incorporators are directors who then admit members and in other jurisdictions they are members who then elect the directors. In yet others there are a group of incorporators and a separate group of directors.

Corporations are useful because of their strength in the areas in which the two previous forms of organization fail. First, they are a formally understood structure governed by a defined set of laws and bylaws. While these rules can become onerous on the organization, they do impart a measure of formality and tend to address almost all circumstances in which the corporation might find itself. So unlike the other organizations, there would rarely be a situation when the corporation is ungovernable for lack of direction.

Second, and perhaps more importantly, a corporation is a separate legal entity from its incorporators. For this reason, the liabilities of the organization are (at least at first) the liabilities of the corporation. For example, a debt owing to a supplier would be a debt of the corporation rather than a debt of the individual directors (assuming of course the contract was completed in the corporate name). Similarly, the revocation tax (explained in Chapter 10) would normally be a debt of the corporation rather than the debt of the directors. This is not to say that the directors can never become responsible for the debts of the corporation. In certain circumstances, the directors may be responsible for source deductions or the unpaid wages of employees or, where directors behave negligently, for the debts of the corporation. (Note that this does not include debts related to improper use of gifts for which the donors have given specific instructions for their use).

JURISDICTION

Creating a corporation depends on the jurisdiction in which the organization plans to make its home base. Within Canada, an organization can be incorporated either federally or through any of the provinces and territories (some provinces have more than one law under which the corporation can be created). When the corporation is created it becomes subject to the regime described in that law under which it is incorporated. While every province has some law dealing with the creation of corporations without shares, the laws in this country are not standardized and so the responsibilities under various laws differ.

It is beyond the scope of this book to detail all the different laws and circumstances in which the corporation may find itself, but it is important to understand that in every province one at least has a choice; one may incorporate either federally or provincially. Nevertheless, a basic outline of the divergences from some of the more important elements of the Canada Not for Profit Act is below.

Canada Not for Profit Corporations Act	
How many people are required to incorporate?	At least one, but soliciting corporations must have a minimum of three directors.
Are the first incorporators members or directors?	The incorporators do not assume either a member or director role by serving as incorporator.
Are there audit requirements? If so, at what level?	Soliciting corporations with less than $50,000 in revenue may have a *unanimous* vote not to have an audit, but they may audit. Soliciting corporations between $50,000 and $250,000 must have a financial review or an audit. Soliciting corporations with greater than $250,000 must have an audit.
What are the costs of incorporating?	Through Industry Canada's online registry system, $200. Otherwise, $250.
What are the costs of filing the annual return?	Through Industry Canada's online registry, $20. Otherwise, $40.

Canada Not for Profit Corporations Act	
Additional Notes	The CNCA distinguishes between soliciting and non soliciting corporations. Soliciting Corporation - Any CNCA corporation that has received in the previous fiscal year greater than $10,000 worth of donations or gifts requested from: • any person who is not a member, director, officer or employee of the corporation at the time of the request (or the spouse or family member of such a person); • grants or similar financial assistance received from the federal government or a provincial or municipal government, or an agency of such a government; or, • donations or gifts of money or other property from a soliciting corporation another corporation or entity that has received income in the manner described above. In addition to lower thresholds for audit requirements, Industry Canada publishes the financial statements of soliciting corporations. Ex officio directors are not permitted.

Alberta Companies Act	
How many people are required to incorporate?	At least 3.
Are the first incorporators members or directors?	Members.
Are there audit requirements? If so, at what level?	Audits are generally required for organizations with over $1,000,000 in revenue and with more than 5 members. Otherwise, in certain circumstances audits can be avoided.
What are the costs of incorporating?	$75
What are the costs of filing the annual return?	No fee for filing.

Alberta Societies Act	
How many people are required to incorporate?	At least five.
Are the first incorporators members or directors?	Members.
Are there audit requirements? If so, at what level?	The by-laws of an Alberta society must contain provisions for the audit of accounts. Audited financial statements must be presented at a society's annual general meeting and signed by the society's auditor, setting out the society's income, disbursements, assets and liabilities and submitted to the government in the annual report.
What are the costs of incorporating?	$50
What are the costs of filing the annual return?	No fee for filing.
Additional Notes	A corporation under the Alberta Societies Act may not have a purpose of carrying on a trade or business (s. 3).

British Columbia Society Act	
How many people are required to incorporate?	At least five.
Are the first incorporators members or directors?	Members.
Are there audit requirements? If so, at what level?	Yes, and no minimal threshold.
What are the costs of incorporating?	$130
What are the costs of filing the annual return?	$25
Additional Notes	The Society Act states that the incorporators may submit up to three proposed names using a name approval request form and a $30 fee.

Manitoba Corporations Act	
How many people are required to incorporate?	At least one
Are the first incorporators members or directors?	Members.
What are the costs of filing the annual return?	$25
Additional Notes	While the word "Manitoba" may not be used as the first word in a corporation with share capital, it can be in a corporation without share capital. The words "Association" or "Society" may also be used only by corporations without share capital.

New Brunswick Companies Act	
How many people are required to incorporate?	At least three.
Are the first incorporators members or directors?	Members.
Are there audit requirements? If so, at what level?	Yes, no minimum required.
What are the costs of incorporating?	Between $50 and $200 depending on the assets of the proposed corporation.
What are the costs of filing the annual return?	$2
Additional Notes	Section 18(2) prohibits a company which falls under its jurisdiction from any business or trade for the profit of its members.

Newfoundland Corporations Act	
How many people are required to incorporate?	At least one.
Are the first incorporators members or directors?	Members.
Are there audit requirements? If so, at what level?	An audit can be dispensed with by unanimous consent of the members.
What are the costs of incorporating?	$70 if filed in paper form, $63 if filed electronically.
What are the costs of filing the annual return?	$0

Nova Scotia Companies Act	
How many people are required to incorporate?	At least one.
Are the first incorporators members or directors?	Members.
Are there audit requirements? If so, at what level?	Yes, no minimum threshold.
What are the costs of incorporating?	$326
What are the costs of filing the annual return?	$36

Nova Scotia Societies Act	
How many people are required to incorporate?	At least five.
Are the first incorporators members or directors?	Members.
Are there audit requirements? If so, at what level?	Must file a financial statement with the Registrar signed by an auditor, if there is one, or two directors otherwise.
What are the costs of incorporating?	$42.35
What are the costs of filing the annual return?	$30.25

Ontario Not-for-Profit Corporations Act	
How many people are required to incorporate?	At least one.
Are the first incorporators members or directors?	First incorporators are not necessarily either first directors or incorporators.
Are there audit requirements? If so, at what level?	A public benefit corporation can pass a resolution to have a review engagement instead of an audit requirement if gross revenue is less than $500,000 (if less than $100,000, can dispense in the same manner with the review engagement). If not a public benefit corporation, it can pass extraordinary resolution to have a review engagement instead of an audit if the corporation has more than $500,000 in annual revenue (if less than $500,000, it can dispense in the same manner with any audit or review engagement).
What are the costs of incorporating?	Not established yet.
What are the costs of filing the annual return?	Currently unknown.
Additional Notes	The Act, when it comes into force, will replace the Corporations Act. Corporations without share capital who previously were under the Corporations Act will have three years to migrate to the new Act. After three years, they will be deemed to be subject to the new legislation. This act is similar to the CNCA in many ways.

PEI Companies Act	
How many people are required to incorporate?	At least three
Are the first incorporators members or directors?	Members. However, at least three of the applicants for the letter patent must become the first directors.
Are there audit requirements? If so, at what level?	Open to specification in the by-laws.
What are the costs of incorporating?	$265
What are the costs of filing the annual return?	$30

Quebec Companies Act	
How many people are required to incorporate?	At least three
Are the first incorporators members or directors?	Members.
Are there audit requirements? If so, at what level?	None.
What are the costs of incorporating?	$107
What are the costs of filing the annual return?	$34 for regular or $60 for priority registration.

Quebec Companies Act	
Additional Notes	Need to search for name of corporation (subject to Quebec language charter and certain limitations), pay fees for the search, and provide a copy of the search at time of registration.

Saskatchewan Non-profit Corporations Act	
How many people are required to incorporate?	At least one.
Are the first incorporators members or directors?	The act requires one incorporator and a separate list of first directors.
Are there audit requirements? If so, at what level?	If charitable corporation, may to have a review engagement instead of an audit requirement if revenue is less than $250,000. If less than $25,000, can dispense in the same manner with the review engagement.
What are the costs of incorporating?	$65
What are the costs of filing the annual return?	$10
Additional Notes	Unless otherwise provided, the directors may make, amend or repeal bylaws. These stay in effect until the next general meeting and must be approved by the members then.

Northwest Territories Societies Act	
How many people are required to incorporate?	At least five.
Are the first incorporators members or directors?	Members.
Are there audit requirements? If so, at what level?	Open to specification in the by-laws.
What are the costs of incorporating?	$50
What are the costs of filing the annual return?	Nil.

Yukon Societies Act	
How many people are required to incorporate?	At least five.
Are the first incorporators members or directors?	There are a separate list of first directors.
Are there audit requirements? If so, at what level?	No specifications for audit in the Act.
What are the costs of incorporating?	$30
What are the costs of filing the annual return?	$10

Incorporating

While there are different laws in every jurisdiction, the process for incorporating is practically the same in all of them. In order to incorporate, a group is generally required of three to five incorporators. These people will serve to be the originators of the corporation. As stated earlier, in some provinces these incorporators are the first directors and in others they are the first members.

An organization will also require charitable objects as described elsewhere in this book, and at the CRA's insistence, it should also contain a dissolution clause. This clause will require that upon dissolution as a corporation the assets of the corporation will be transferred to other qualified donees. It bears mentioning that an organization will probably lose its charitable status before dissolution. In such a circumstance, by operation of the revocation tax, the organization will already have distributed all of its assets, and as a result the organization will have no assets left for distribution when it is dissolved as a corporation. Alternatively, it may have distributed all of its assets at the time of deregistration but then built up additional assets *after* deregistration but before dissolution as a corporation. If that is the case, then the organization may wish to revisit the dissolution clause after its revocation as a charity in order that it may distribute its assets in a different manner. Organizations that are contemplating a dissolution clause may also seek to limit the clause in order that assets be distributed out to organizations with similar charitable objects.

Unfortunately it is impossible to conduct a thorough review of each of the various laws in the different provinces which may apply to organizations seeking incorporation. However, organizations may wish to approach the decision with some forethought as certain laws have certain requirements which they may find undesirable. For example, certain laws require audits at different financial thresholds. Given that audits are expensive, an organization might wish to seek a higher threshold at which it must seek the audit. Some laws are less vigorous in their governance requirements while others may make amalgamation or continuance into another law difficult or impossible. For this reason qualified counsel should be sought out that can help advise a prospective corporation about the different regimes which may be available to the organization.

Maintenance

Corporations are designed to be "living" entities which means that they require maintenance in order that their operations and decisions are legally valid. Most of the obligations are apparent from a thorough reading of the bylaws and statute. For example, organizations require a meeting of the members which allows the members to elect the directors. Another provision may indicate that directors have term limits and so should not be occupying their position any longer than is allowed.

In another vein, organizations have legal requirements imposed upon them by statute. For example, there may be a corporate information return to be filed every year including the names of all the directors and their addresses. For example, the Canada Not-For Profit Corporations Act requires that each director of the corporation be known to the government and that the government be informed within fifteen days of a move of the residential address of any of the directors.

The actual maintenance requirements of each corporation depends, perhaps obviously, on the law under which it was incorporated, but it can be assumed that:

- each entity is required to have a meeting
- the members must be admitted properly to the corporation
- the directors must be properly elected
- there must be an annual meeting of the members each year allowing the members to review the financial statements, elect the directors and appoint the auditors if required

It is important that the bylaws be read and consulted each time there is a meeting or any time there is doubt about how the corporation should operate. Many times we have seen people simply assume that bylaws were "suggestions" or that they could be safely ignored. This is not the case. Bylaws have been developed over time by people with experience in the operations of corporations. They are meant to be followed *in all circumstances*. The trouble with ignoring the bylaws for the sake of expediency is that eventually the corporation runs into a situation where the legal validity of a decision of the corporation may be questioned. If the bylaws had been followed properly up to that time, then there can be no doubt that the decisions of the corporation taken are legally valid. However, there are circumstances where a step missed forty years previous can affect the legal validity of a decision today. For this reason we recommend that bylaws and statutes be consulted consistently in order to ensure that decisions are properly made.

Dissolution

Eventually the time may come when the corporation is to be dissolved. Generally, the process by which the dissolution may take place is outlined within the organizing statute. However, dissolution of corporations must be made in consultation with the relevant legal regime (this is generally the law under which the corporation was originally incorporated).

Assuming that an organization has already met its charity law obligations after revocation, the revocation tax rules would likely operate to make the corporation an empty shell, in these circumstances the dissolution process is fairly simple. Typically it involves the filing of dissolution documents with the relevant government ministry and certain public notices. This in itself necessitates that the organization has filed all the necessary tax documents and owes no money to the government or anyone else. In these circumstances the corporation can be dissolved.

If the corporation is not dissolved and simply exists as a moribund entity, the liabilities of the directors may continue. Generally, potential liabilities of the corporation and its directors will cease after a certain time period. The time period often starts to run when the directors cease to act as such. For some directors (usually those left unable to find their own replacements – like a corporate version of musical chairs, the ones left standing when the music stops) this may require dissolution of the corporation in order that the timeline can begin. Therefore, some directors may want to ensure that the corporation is properly dissolved as early as possible.

In certain circumstances, usually involuntary to the directors, the corporation may be dissolved at the behest of the government. Generally this happens when the corporation fails to file proper documentation with the relevant government ministry. In these circumstances the corporation may be informed by that office that it no longer exists as a corporation. When this happens, and if the organization is a registered charity, it will become liable to the revocation tax. Thus, missing a filing may result not only in loss of corporate status it may also result in the loss of charitable status and the loss of all the assets of the corporation as well.

Amalgamation

At times, corporations may seek out others with a similar mandate to gain efficiencies by amalgamating the two entities. Amalgamations of such corporations can be somewhat difficult because the laws that govern these corporations can be outdated and contain insufficient legal means to effect an amalgamation. Of course, this assumes that both corporations are governed by the same law. Where the corporations exist under different laws it may be necessary to continue one of them into the others act (if possible) so that an amalgamation is possible.

In the world of registered charities, amalgamations are rare. The transfer of assets between registered charities can be effected rather simply and since the membership of such entities can expand without much difficulty, "mergers" are generally conducted as transfers of assets from one entity to another and subscription of new members to the combined. In either case, the amalgamation should not be attempted without the benefit of advice from counsel experienced in this area.

OPERATING EXTRA- PROVINCIALLY

Many entities operate in more than one province. It would be too easy to assume that they could do so without complying with some additional laws. In fact, each province will assert some new law which may make operations in that province more complicated. For example, operating in Quebec requires a separate Quebec charitable registration number. Operating in Alberta or Saskatchewan may require registration under one of the fundraising acts and operation in Ontario requires certain compliance with the office of the Ontario Public Guardian and Trustee. To make matters worse, creating a base of operations in any of the provinces may require specific filings. Thus, an organization may be subjected to filings in each of the various provinces simply because it has a base of operations as defined by that province's legislation.

As outlined in the following charts, it is only corporations which must file the documentation relating to extra-provincial corporations. The rules for fundraising and charitable registration at the office of the Ontario Public Guardian and Trustee apply to all entities regardless of whether or not they are incorporated.

British Columbia -

Extra-provincial registration

Applications are given to the Registrar of Companies and may be granted a certificate of registration. Certification may have conditions of registration with it. Detailed information is available in the notice "Information for Registration of an Extra-provincial Society." The application fee is $100.00.

Steps to extra-provincial registration

1. Apply for approval of the extra-provincial society's name (details below). This is not required if the society is a federal corporation.

2. File a Statement on Registration of Extra-provincial Society with copies of the certified incorporating documents, a statement of good standing from the incorporating body and a certified copy of the society's by-laws.

3. File the constitution and by-laws using either Form 1, if using the bylaws set out in Schedule B of the Society Act; Form 2, if adapting the Schedule B bylaws with changes or additions or Form 3, if using a customized set of bylaws for the society.

4. File the List of First Directors using Form 4 and Notice of Address of Society using Form 5. These can be filed either online or by mail.

5. The society must file an application for appointment of an attorney if they have not already done so.

6. The Registrar will assess the application and either issue the certificate of registration or refuse it. If granted, registration will be published and copies will be sent to the society's head office and appointed attorneys.

Unless the registrar otherwise provides, the extra-provincial society must comply with the laws relating to by-laws, names, constituting provisions and any changes therein.

Names

Extra-provincial corporations (societies) must request to reserve their corporate name. This can be done either:

- online
- at a Government Agent's office
- at an OneStop service delivery location
- by a BC OnLine account
- by mail

You may submit three name choices to the Names Examiner of the Registrar of Companies. The filing fee online is $31.58 and by mail is $30.00. A name will be reserved for 56 calendar days. If all your submitted names are rejected, a society must restart the process with three new submissions.

Appointed Attorney

Once the certificate of registration is granted, the extra-provincial society must appoint a person resident in British Columbia to act as its attorney for service, authorized and directed by the society to accept all legal notices and proceedings brought to, by, or against the society. Within a week after this appointment, the society must file the appointment – including name and contact information – with the registrar and no more than a week may pass between the termination of the first and any subsequent appointments. Any changes to the appointment require a notice of change to be filed with the registrar.

Maintaining an extra-provincial society

To maintain an extra-provincial registration, the society must file:

- A verified copy of amendments to the constitution and by-laws within a month of any taking place. Each change requires a $15.00 filing fee.
- Any changes to the address of the head office, directors (Form 7) or the addresses (Form 5), name or attorney for service. Each filing requires a $15.00 filing fee.
- The Annual Report (Form 11), filed within thirty days of each general meeting; a $25.00 fee applies.

These forms may be submitted by mail to:

> **Ministry of Finance**
> BC Registry of Services
> PO Box 9431
> Stn Prov Govt,
> Victoria BC V8W 9V3

Alberta -

Application documents

The Corporation should apply to the Registrar by submitting certified copies, in English, of the following documents:

- a Statement of Registration
- a certified copy of the charter (letter of incorporation, and any supplementary letters patent)
- the name or operating name and the NUANS Alberta Search Report
- the appointment of an attorney for service and if applicable, the alternative attorney for service; their name and address

Once the application is complete, applicants should submit it to an authorized service provider who will examine the application and confer upon the organization a Certificate of Registration. Authorized service providers are private sector firms that have levels of accreditation for the number of services they provide. Service fees are not regulated by the government and so there may be price differentials between authorized service providers.

Name

The corporation's name must conform to the requirements of a corporate name under the Alberta Business Corporations Act regulations. The name also:

- must not be prohibited;
- must not be identical or similar (confusing or misleading) to another corporation incorporated in Alberta or federally, or another extra-provincial corporation continued in Alberta.

The Registrar may approve of the use of an operating name should there be a conflict, and this operating name may be cancelled at any time. Under the operating name the corporation may incur the rights, debts and liabilities as if it were registered under its real name. The corporation may be sued under its own name, its operating name, or both.

Attorney

Every extra-provincial corporation must appoint for itself an attorney for service to represent the corporation in Alberta. The attorney need not be a lawyer. Upon death or resignation of an appointed attorney, the extra-provincial corporation must appoint another and register the appointment.

Maintaining the registration

Amendments

A registered corporation must send to the Register through an authorized service provider:

- certified copies of all amendments filed in the home jurisdiction within one month of their taking effect
- notices of change if the attorney, directors, office address, or directors' addresses change

Annual Returns

The corporation must render annual returns to the Registrar no later than the last day of the anniversary month of its incorporation in the other jurisdiction. The form is available online.

- No act of the extra-provincial corporation will be invalid only by reason of the corporation not being registered or the act being contrary or unauthorized by the charter of the corporation or laws of the incorporating jurisdiction.

Fundraising

Charitable fundraising, conducted by professional fundraisers and also charities themselves, is regulated by the *Charitable Fund-raising Act*. Charities, whether incorporated or not, must register if they make solicitations for contributions and if:

- they use a fund-raising business to solicit contributions;
- they intend to raise more than $25,000 in gross contributions in its financial year from solicitations of individuals in Alberta; or
- they raised more than $25,000 in gross contributions in its financial year in which case they must register within 45 days of receiving $25,000 in gross contributions.

Depending on the organizational and operational structure of the extra-provincial charity, it may be exempt from the above restrictions. For example, no registration is required by an unincorporated charity group that is affiliated with another organization and the affiliate controls the distributions of the contributions the charity receives during the financial year.

- Only charities registered under the ACFA can employ a fundraising business to solicit contributions on its behalf.
- A charity *must* register if their solicitations are:
- direct or indirect requests for contribution where it is stated or implied that it will be used by a charitable organization or purpose (keeping in mind the broad definition of such under the ACFA); or
- requests for contribution through a direct or indirect request to buy goods or services through which it is stated or implied that some or the entire purchase price will be used by a charitable organization or purpose.

A charity *does not need* to register if their solicitations are only:

- made by a member of a charity to their family members;
- for goods or services used by the charity for a non-charitable (ex: administrative) purposes; or
- through a licensed gaming activity such as raffles, bingos or casinos.

Steps to register a charity for fundraising purposes:

1. Fill out the Application for Charitable Organization and fee ($60.00).
2. If registering for the first time, submit copies of solicitation materials and telemarketing scripts that will be used for fundraising.

Registration is for one year. Further information is available through Service Alberta online.

Donors' rights

If a charity conducts solicitations with intent to gross more than $25,000 in a financial year, it is required to provide, upon request by donors, copies of recently audited financial statements, the portion of gross contributions received that were used directly for the charitable purposes of the charity, reasonable detail about where and how the contributions it solicits will be spent and other information required by the regulations. All contributions made in the course of solicitations must be receipted if requested, except for the direct or indirect requests to buy goods.

Receipting and record-keeping

Charities must keep complete financial records for fundraising activities going back at least three years.

These include:

- original financial statements
- records of all solicitations;

- records of the bank account (if any) used for deposits and any payments from that account
- names of the signing officers for the bank account
- samples of the information given to potential donors, including publications and phone scripts
- copies of the fund-raising agreement and any amendments
- copies of cash receipts

Saskatchewan -

The application should include:

- the fee ($115 for a paper filing)
- copy of the articles of incorporation
- a power of attorney

The Director will also require a Request for Name Availability Search and Reservation.

Power of attorney

The corporation is required to name and register an individual residing in Saskatchewan in a power of attorney unless the corporation has a director or officer resident in Saskatchewan.

Name

A corporation should apply to reserve its name or alternate name through the "Request for Name Availability Search and Reservation Form." Any alternative trade name must be registered under the *Business Names Registration Act*.

Changes

The corporation must notify the Director within fifteen days of any changes in address of head office, attorney, or directors. Copies of any articles of amendment must also be sent to the Director.

Annual return

The corporation must file an annual return with the Director.

Fundraising

Charities should be aware of the rules regarding solicitations for contributions whether by phone, telephone, door-to-door or another form. The latter may include operating a web site that solicits, or receives contributions from Saskatchewan residents. Telephone and door-to-door solicitations are allowed between 8:00 am and 9:00 pm. Contributions may be for money, services or goods, or any pledge or promise for contributions.

If a charity hires a fundraising business to solicit on its behalf, the business must be licensed under the *Charitable Fund-raising Businesses Act* (the "CFBA"). The fundraising agreement must be in writing and in the manner and form prescribed in the Act which requires that the Agreement:

(a) must be in writing;

(b) must include:
(i) all the terms and conditions between the parties respecting the fund-raising, including:
(A) the duties and responsibilities of both parties; and
(B) the manner in which the fund-raising agreement may be terminated;

(ii) an estimate of the amount of contributions to be received and an estimate of the expenses and costs of the fund-raising;

(iii) if the solicitations will involve selling goods or services, a description of
the goods or services and the specific price for which the goods or services
will be sold;

(iv) the address of:
(A) the charitable organization; and
(B) the licensee;

(v) the name and telephone number of the contact person for:
(A) the charitable organization; and
(B) the licensee; and

(vi) any other prescribed matter; and

(c) must set out:
(i) the solicitation method or methods to be used;
(ii) the remuneration of the licensee, being either or a combination of the following:
(A) a specified amount of money;
(B) a specified percentage of gross contributions; and
(iii) the method by which the remuneration is to be paid.

(3) Every licensee that enters into a fundraising agreement pursuant to subsection (1) shall provide a copy of that agreement to the registrar within the prescribed period prior to commencing a campaign of solicitation.

To any person from whom they are requesting a contribution, a charity must provide (amongst other things):

- the remuneration being paid to the third party fundraiser
- various contact information of the organization on whose behalf of the donations are being solicited
- the charitable purpose for which the donations are being used
- the jurisdiction in which the funds will be spent

They must also provide to anyone who requests it:

- copies of recent financial statements
- the portion of gross revenues that were used on charitable purposes in the last year
- an estimate of the amount that will be used on charitable purposes in the current year
- information about where and how the revenues are spent, and information regarding any fundraising businesses used

Manitoba -

Extra-provincial registration

Philanthropic non-share capital corporations (i.e. charities) must register under the *Corporations Act* of Manitoba in order to conduct business in Manitoba. Registration with the Companies Office accords the entity with legal personality. Registration is valid for three years and may be renewed by the registrant; otherwise, the business name will be cancelled. The Application for Registration fee is $120.

All the necessary forms for registration, renewal and changes are available online.

Name

Charities may reserve a name online at a fee of $45 and payment is by credit card only.

- The name should consist of a distinctive element, a descriptive element, and end with a legal element (for corporate name only).

- The name should not be confusingly similar to an existing name or trademark.
- The name must not be objectionable.

The charity must provide the reason for the reservation, the name, the nature of the business and the location of the business and all other relevant information. For extra-provincial and federal registrations, if the name is in both French and English there is only need for one registration.

With every document submitted, whether to register, renew or change, a "Request for Service Form" must be submitted as well.

Maintaining registration

Changes -

- Change of business name ($45.00 fee applies),
- Change of address (no fee), and
- Change of directors (no fee) declaration must be given to the Companies Office as applicable.

Annual return

An extra-provincial or federally registered charity must file annual returns in Manitoba, at a cost of $25.00 for non-share capital corporations. It should be filed as of the last day of the anniversary month every year.

Registration of unincorporated associations

An unincorporated organization may submit a "Request for Name Notation" in order to establish a presence in the Companies Office records for three years and can be changed or renewed or dissolved thereafter. The unincorporated association still must reserve and register its business name.

Ontario -

Extra-provincial registration

Registration is completed by filing an "Initial Return" (Form 2) with the Central Production and Verification Services Branch at 393 University Ave, Suite 200, Toronto, Ontario M5G 2M2 within sixty days of carrying on the activities in Ontario. Non-share capital corporations must include in the Initial Return:

- the name of the corporation
- the Ontario corporation number
- the date of the incorporation/amalgamation, whichever is more recent
- the name of the jurisdiction of incorporation/amalgamation referred to above
- address of the corporation's head or registered office

- the date the corporation commenced activities in Ontario and/or ceased (if any)
- name and office address of the chief officer or manager in Ontario, if any and the date they assumed the role, and/or when it ceased
- address of the principle office in Ontario
- if the corporation is required to have an agent for service in Ontario, the contact information for the agent and the Ontario corporation number if the agent is a corporation
- preferred language of communication
- the immediate former name of the corporation

An extra-provincial corporation must file a "Notice of Change Form" (Form 2) if any information on the initial return changes. A copy of the form is available at **www.runningacharity.ca.**

An extra-provincial corporation can use any name other than its corporate name, except if that name in Ontario is prohibited by the regulations, is the same or similar to an existing organization or individual in Ontario, or would be likely to deceive the public. To ensure that there is no confusion with existing names, corporations should conduct an "Enhanced Business Name Search." It is recommended that the corporation contact a search house to conduct an Ontario NUANS name search report.

Acquiring property in Ontario

Within one month of acquisition, corporations that are charities must report to the Office of the Public Guardian and Trustee (PGT) certain donations given to it, such as real or personal property, or interests therein, or the proceeds vested in an executor or trustee for a charitable purpose trust. Although there is a set form for this report, the notice to the PGT should include:

- a statement of the nature of the property
- a copy of the instrument of conveyance
- detailed information about the corporation

Quebec -

Extra-provincial registration

Registrants must file a Declaration of Registration. This is done via an online form. Paper forms can be attained by contacting Services Quebec at 1-800-361-9596.

Fee for not-for-profit corporations if filed within 60 days of beginning operations in Quebec:

- Regular: no fee
- Priority: $17.00

Fee if filed after the 60 day period:

- Regular: $34.00
- Priority: $51.00

As part of the process, the registrant must submit a “Name Research Report Application” and “Name Reservation Application.”

The corporate name:

- must conform to the Charter of the French languages
- must be reserved
- cannot be prohibited
- cannot be misleading

In addition, the corporation must declare a French version of the name used in Quebec and use the name in association with the activities unless it is only a surname and given name.

Maintaining the registration

Registrants must file an Annual Declaration every year. This is done via an online form. Paper forms can be attained by contacting Services Quebec at 1-800-361-9596.

The Annual Declaration should be filed between May 15 and November 15.

Fee for not-for-profit corporations if filed on time:

- Regular: no fee
- Priority: $17

Fee if filed late:

- Regular: $17
- Priority: $34

Registrants must also notify the enterprises registrar of any amendments during the year. Amending Declarations are at no cost unless a registrant opts for priority processing, in which case a $17.00 fee applies.

Charitable registration

Charities registered federally must nevertheless register with the province of Quebec to issue receipts valid in that province for provincial income tax purposes. This applies whether the organization is incorporated, unincorporated or a trust. The charity should file the Form TP-985.5, “Demande d’enregistrement – Organismes de bienfaisance, institutions muséales, organismes culturels ou de communication et associations québécoises ou canadiennes de sport amateur.” If a charity received federal registration after 2006, applicants must submit their federal registration certificate as well using Form TP-985.22. Normally, registration in Quebec will be automatic once the organization is registered federally.

New Brunswick -

Extra-provincial registration

Where an extra-provincial corporation carries on business in New Brunswick without a purpose of profit, the Director at Service New Brunswick may exempt the corporation from corporate registration requirements under the Business Corporations Act. If an extra-provincial corporation chooses to register, it must do so within thirty days of carrying on business in New Brunswick (NB). Registration gives the corporation the power to commence or maintain any proceedings or actions in a NB court. A proceeding may be maintained if the corporation becomes registered during the proceedings.

If the corporation chooses to apply for the exemption, it should submit the following:

1. A letter indicating that the corporation does not carry on business for the purpose of gain and that it wishes to apply for an exemption.
2. A copy of incorporation documents and any amendments.
3. Form 25, Appointment of Attorney for Service, naming a resident of New Brunswick as its agent.
4. Form 25.1, Consent to Act as Attorney for Service.
5. Fee of $100 payable to Service New Brunswick.

If the corporation instead chooses to register, it must submit:

1. Form 26, Statement of Registration Extra-Provincial Corporation (in duplicate).
2. Form 24, Appointment of Attorney for Service (in duplicate).
3. Form 25.1, Consent to Act as Attorney for Service (in duplicate).
4. The “Additional Information Form.”
5. A copy of the incorporation documents.
6. A New Brunswick NUANS name reservation report generated in the last 90 days.
7. Fee of $212.00 (or $312.00 for expedited service) payable to Service New Brunswick.

Name

An extra-provincial corporation cannot be registered under a name that is:

- deceptively similar to an existing business name without license
- prohibited
- reserved for another business

If it must change its name, the extra-provincial corporation may submit the form "Certificate of Business Name or Renewal of Business Name" and the "Additional Information Form" pursuant to the *Partnerships and Business Names-Registration Act*. Applicants should conduct a NUANS name search report no more than 90 days prior to filing for a name. A Certificate of Business Name costs $112.00 and the Renewal of Business Name costs $62.00.

The government should be notified of any change of name through Form 32.1 "Notice of Change of Name" to the Director to reserve a name for an extra-provincial corporation for ninety days.

Maintaining the registration

Attorney for service -

The attorney must notify the corporation and Director within sixty days if he or she intends to resign. The new appointment must be sent to the Director. A $50.00 fee applies to appoint or change an attorney for service.

Changes -

The registered extra-provincial corporation must notify the Director of any change in its name and the resulting amendment of its constituting documents. A $112.00 fee applies to change the name, or $212.00 or expedited service. As well, within one month of any changes, the Director must be notified of any changes in: the address in NB and the membership of the charity's board of directors or governing body. A nominal fee applies for online processing.

Annual Returns -

The registered extra-provincial corporation must file annual returns with the Director. The charity should use the appropriate form or may also file with it its annual return from the incorporating jurisdiction. The charity may elect to make its anniversary month the same as its incorporating month. A $25.00 fee applies to select an anniversary month. To file online an annual fee of $200.00 applies or $220.00 for a paper filing by mail.

Nova Scotia -

Extra-provincial registration

There is no legislation specifically requiring an extra-provincial charity to register as an entity in Nova Scotia in order to acquire legal status. In conversation with Representatives of the Registry of Joint Stock Companies, it was advised that an extra-provincial charity incorporate in Nova Scotia if it wants to acquire property, open a bank account or obtain insurance etc. Information about incorporating as a society is available online or by contacting the Registry of Joint Stock Companies at 1-800-225-8227.

Prince Edward Island -

Name

Extra-provincial corporations may request a business name by contacting the Consumer, Corporate and Insurance Services Division. The cost of the NUANS name search and registration for three years is $105 payable to the Provincial Treasurer of PEI. The cost of renewal is $50 for each subsequent three-year period.

Steps to registration

1. Request a NUANS name search to reserve a business name.
2. Submit the "Application for Registration" and the fee of $250.

This can be mailed to:

> **The Office of the Attorney General, Consumer,**
> Corporate and Insurance Services
> PO Box 2000,
> Charlottetown, PEI
> CIA 7N8

It can also be submitted in person to:

> 95 Rochford Street
> 4th floor
> Charlottetown, PEI
> C1A 3T6.

Maintaining the registration

Registrants may renew their certificate of registration within six months of the expiration of the most recent certificate by filing a notice of renewal of registration to the Director.

Notify the Director of any changes within 30 days of a change in name, or amalgamation.

Newfoundland and Labrador -

Unlike other provinces which allow a certain period between commencing operations and registration, in Newfoundland and Labrador (NL) the registration must take place *before* operations can be commenced in the province.

In order to register a corporation must:

- File Statement for Registration – Extra-Provincial Company Form 24.
- File a Power of Attorney Form 26.
- File a Statutory Declaration Form 25, attesting to truth of registration and include in the application two certified copies of the statute, certificate or other constituting document of the corporation.
- Pay a fee of $260.

Maintaining the registration

To maintain the registration the corporation must:

- file the Annual Return – Extra-Provincial Company Form 28 with the $200 fee (or $180 if filing online);
- notify the Commercial Registrations Division of any changes in head office by filing the Notice of Change of Chief Place of Business Form 32;
- notify of any change in the registered office in NL by filing the Notice of Change of Registered Office in Newfoundland and Labrador;
- notify of any changes in the power of attorney should the attorney change;
- within one month, notify of any changes in the name of the registrant, in the constituting documents or in the objects of the company.

Name

The name of the extra-provincial corporation must be displayed or affixed outside the head office in NL. There is no independent business name registration in Newfoundland.

Yukon -

Steps to registering

Within thirty days of carrying on business in the Yukon the corporation must:

- appoint an attorney for service;
- notify the registrar of the address of the head office in the incorporating jurisdiction;

- file a Statement of Registration with the $300 fee; and
- reserve a business name or assumed name if the business name is prohibited.

The NUANS name search costs $40.00 and the reservation of an assumed name costs $75.00.

Name

The name should be distinctive, i.e.: not the same or similar to a business name already registered with Corporate Affairs in the Yukon. It should also indicate a legal element. Once registered, applicants should file the "Declaration of Business Name Form."

Maintaining the registration

In order to maintain the registration the corporation must:

- keep up to date records by notifying the registrar of any changes, amendments have a fee of $75;
- if necessary, amend the Registration for an additional $75; and
- file an Annual Return ($15) on or before the last day of the anniversary month (the month in which the corporation became subject to the YBCA).

Northwest Territories -

Steps to registering

In order to register a corporation must:

- conduct a name search and reserve request if the corporation is not federally incorporated for a $25.00 fee;
- send to the Registrar a certified copy of the constituting documents of the corporation and any amendments;
- provide a certificate of no more than thirty days old of the good standing of the corporation in the incorporating jurisdiction;
- register the address of the corporation by filing, in duplicate, Form 21 "Notice of Registered Office" or "Notice of Change of Registered Office Extra-Territorial Corporation";
- submit Form 18 "Statement of Registration Extra-Territorial Corporation;" and,
- pay the filing fee of $100.

The Department of Justice, Corporate Registry has informational booklets on filling out the required forms available online.

Registration of extra-territorial corporate name

Except for a federally incorporated corporation, there are restrictions on the name of the business. It must not contain prohibited words as per the NWTBCA Regulations, is not the same or misleadingly similar to an existing registered corporation in the NWT, and is not a reserved name. If there is no problem with the name, the Registry will reserve the name for 90 days.

Maintaining the registration

Registered extra-provincial corporations should:

- maintain a registered office in the NWT at all times, that is accessible to the public during normal business hours;
- within thirty days, inform the government of any changes in the address, name, or constituting documents and be provided with certified copies; and
- file an annual return with the Registrar in the anniversary month of the incorporation or amalgamations.

Nunavut -

Extra-territorial registration

The legislation and requirements are the same as those under the Northwest Territories *Business Corporations Act* except that the certificate of status is not required in Nunavut. Registrations are filed with the Department of Justice, Legal Registries Division (Corporate Registry).

3

What is a Charity?

Most Canadians understand that a charity is an organization that undertakes good deeds for the benefit of others or some cause understood to be charitable, however, the legal meaning of charity differs from the understood lay meaning and an organization seeking registered charity status with the CRA will not succeed without complying with the legal meaning. This chapter is intended to review the legal basis for which an organization can qualify to be a charity.

The law does not assume that every organization that undertakes a cause for the public benefit is necessarily a charity. Fundamentally, if an organization wants to qualify as a charity under Canadian law it has two choices: either it finds a case which found that the cause in question was charitable in law, or it falls under some legal mechanism which effectively gives the organization the same benefits as other registered charities.

Of course, it is beyond the scope of this book to detail every case that has been decided in this area over the past 400 years and so in this chapter we present a summarized version of the law. An organization interested in undertaking work in some *novel* area related to a cause already understood to be charitable should contact qualified legal counsel.

CHARITIES VS NOT-FOR-PROFIT VS FOR-PROFIT

A registered charity is defined in the Income Tax Act as one formed for charitable purposes; but there is no statutory definition of "charitable purposes." As discussed in the introduction, a charitable purpose is one where a court has found that the cause to be undertaken falls within what the law understands to be charitable. Not all charities necessarily must be registered as such with the CRA.

It is important to understand that a not-for-profit is different from a charity, and different rules apply to such an organization. A not-for-profit is one which is *not a charity at law* but (like a charity) will not provide certain benefits (generally payments) to the members of the group. Political groups and recreational organizations are typically not-for-profits. While in common parlance a not-for-profit and a charity are considered interchangeable, they are *not* the same thing and charities should be careful about referring to themselves as a not-for-profit as it implies that the group cannot issue charitable donation tax receipts.

A for-profit organization is one which is neither a not-for-profit nor a registered charity. Organizations should take care that they are not an unregistered charity as such groups might find themselves falling within the definition of for-profit organizations for tax purposes. Such organizations are subject to tax on *all* of their income and of course cannot issue charitable donation tax receipts.

OTHER QUALIFIED DONEES

Canadians understand that donations to registered charities result in tax receipts which can be used to create donation tax credits on their income tax returns. However, registered charities are only one of several groups which can issue tax receipts. These organizations are called qualified donees. The list includes the following types of organizations:

a. Registered Charities
b. Registered Canadian Amateur Athletic Associations
c. The United Nations or an agency of the United Nations
d. Federal, Provincial or municipal governments, or a public body performing a function of government (generally refers to the government of an Indian reserve)
e. Certain not-for-profit housing corporations
f. Certain foreign universities listed in Schedule VIII to the Income Tax Act Regulations
g. Certain other foreign organizations that have been granted this status

The actual list of prescribed universities worldwide is very long and includes most of the universities in the USA and most other universities which have at least some Canadian students. There is a process available for universities that wish to be included on this list. Such universities should contact qualified legal counsel if they seek to be included.

The list of organizations to which the government gives gifts to in a year is generally shrouded in secrecy. It is clear that the government has allowed itself the ability to include some foreign organizations but traditionally the decision as to how such organizations get included on the list has been difficult to ascertain. It would be unlikely that any organization could simply "wish" to be included on this list and arrange for it to happen without some compelling reason for the government to involve itself in this arrangement.

CHARITABLE OBJECTS

The purposes for which a charity must be organized are known as charitable objects. They can be found in the organizing documents of every type of charitable entity. Typically, these statements serve to limit the organization's ability to engage in any activity other than what is included in the objects. Over the past 400 years the law in this area has been divided into four categories, or heads. A proposed object that does not fall within one of the four heads is not eligible for registration.

There are two fundamental elements to a charitable object. The first is that the object itself must be found to have been charitable at law in a previous case, or the object must otherwise be analogous to some previously decided case. The second element is that the manner in which the object is to be fulfilled must be for the public benefit. It is not sufficient that the cause to be undertaken is to benefit the public - it must meet the element of having been decided to be charitable at law.

Entities will only get registered as charities if their objects allow them to pursue charitable purposes and nothing but charitable purposes. The CRA will also refuse registration where it finds that the entity has an unstated collateral purpose as evidenced by the entity's activities. So, it is important that the objects be broad enough to encompass the organization's activities but tightly worded to prevent the organization from pursuing activities which would not qualify as charitable. For this reason most successful organizations have between one and four objects and no more.

It is important to note that that the objects need not contain a list of every constituent activity necessary to accomplish the final objective. For example, objects never include things like buying vegetables when the overall purpose is to feed the hungry. Necessary components and ancillary activities to pursuing the object need not be mentioned. On the other hand, the CRA generally does require some limiting wording in the object which defines the activity to be undertaken in pursuit of the charitable activity; for example, to relieve poverty by teaching vocational skills – rather than simply 'to relieve poverty'. The CRA also generally prefers a clause stating the eligible beneficiary group, although from a technical perspective this is often unnecessary.

Properly drafted charitable objects are critical to a successful application for registered charity status. It is not sufficient to rely on the fact that there are other organizations out there that do similar work, or to provide a listing of the things you intend for the organization to do. Rather, a considered, researched approach should be employed to ensure that the charity has the right to do what it needs – and to give the CRA confidence that the organization is deserving of registration.

CHARITABLE HEADS

Advancement of education

Advancement of education is perhaps the most controversial of charitable heads. Technically, advancing education in the charitable sense means formally training the mind, advancing the knowledge or abilities of the recipient, or improving the useable branch of human knowledge. This would involve running a school, conducting and publishing research or providing academic scholarships to attend university.

Advancing education does not mean convincing others of a position. This argument has been rejected several times by the Courts in looking at issues of abortion. The law is clear on the point that there is no room to define education as being one where a charity ostensibly tries to "educate" others of its position.

Generally speaking, education should be understood in an almost antiseptic way. Typical educational programs which teach the basics of science, language, math and the social sciences qualify. This does not mean that taking a position on a side in an academic debate is prohibited, rather that both elements of the academic debate must be presented to the students.

Organizations that seek charitable status under this head will be asked by the CRA for confirmation of the curriculum, the qualifications of the teachers and the facilities and the students which will receive the education. Such groups should typically provide the type of education that one would expect to find in most schools and universities on topics that are generally offered in these organizations. Continuing education programs for adults will also qualify so long as the education is not intended to further the recipients' professional earnings and otherwise meets the restrictions placed on charities operating in this area.

Advancement of religion

Advancing religion in the charitable sense means manifesting, promoting, sustaining or increasing belief in a religion. To qualify as a religion there must be faith in a higher unseen power such as a god, supreme being or entity; worship or reverence; and a particular and comprehensive system of doctrines and observances.

The key element to the advancement of religion is the requirement that there be an element of theistic worship. Judaism, Christianity, Islam, Buddhism, Hinduism and Taoism all have organizations registered in Canada. There are however some notable exceptions including Scientology, Jainism and Shinto. While it may be offensive that in today's multicultural Canada there are some religious groups which do not qualify for registered charity status there is little the CRA can do to change this. The only substantive change to this policy will come when the issue is litigated to the Federal Court of Appeal by an organization refused registration as a charity.

Nevertheless, given the sensitivity of the issue, officers of the Charities Directorate have been known to bend over backwards to find some other grounds upon which to register groups which do not meet the technical definition of the advancement of religion.

Typically organizations that advance religion will be ones that are involved in missionary work or outreach, operation of a church, synagogue, or temple with regular worship services, or the conduct of religious schools.

Relief of poverty

Relieving poverty means providing relief for the poor and not only the destitute. "Poor" is defined as anyone lacking essential amenities available to the general public. The test of amenities available to the general public does not necessarily mean that if an individual in a poor region lacks clean water as does everyone else in that region, that the provision of clean water is not charitable as no one in the area has it. Rather, it is understood that there are certain basic requirements of life that everyone needs. Providing these requirements is charitable. Examples include providing food and basic health care, tuition subsidies for low-income individuals and micro-loan financing so that the poor can set up their own businesses.

Generally speaking there is a presumption of public benefit for the relief of poverty. This means that the CRA will not usually question the public benefit nature of the relief of poverty. Nevertheless, if an organization seems to be relieving poverty within a certain group or amongst a certain predefined set of people, the CRA may question whether the purpose of the group is to provide funds to a private group.

The organizations set up to relieve poverty are typically food banks, shelters, and even many missionary groups which provide the basis of life to the poor in developing parts of the world.

Certain other purposes beneficial to the community in a way the law regards as charitable

This heading is not a basket clause to include every other activity that Canadians may want to undertake as registered charities. Rather, it is a broad description of those purposes that do not fall under any of the first three heads but which a court has decided is charitable. There are a number of examples, including hospitals, museums, various children's causes, various seniors' causes, advancing the public's appreciation of the arts, and helping immigrants. There are literally hundreds of years' worth of cases which have been decided all over the Commonwealth which directly affect the types of organizations which may qualify as charitable under this head.

Prospective organizations typically see some other charity operating in this area and understand that they too may qualify. Given that this area of law is often argued by analogy, such reasoning is sound. Clearly, an organization which seeks registration under this head of charity must ask a lawyer with experience in this area to find another case on which the organization can hang its metaphorical hat. You will learn more about this in the section on model objects.

Organizations that seek registration under this head of charity may find the object for which they seek to be organized defined under that section. Assuming that is the case, the work such organizations will have to undertake in order to draft proper objects is already done for them. Therefore, any organization seeking registration in this area may first want to review the model objects put out by the CRA and, if possible, the objects of other organizations which they intend to emulate.

CRA INTERPRETATIONS

Because the development of the law in this area by the courts takes place at a glacial pace (if at all), over the years the CRA has taken the opportunity to express its position on its interpretation of existing law. These interpretations often have the net effect of advancing the law by allowing organizations to engage in activities in ways that would not be clear by a simple reading of the *Income Tax Act* and case law. Any organization seeking registration (or actually operating) in these areas should review the relevant guidance. The CRA currently has published guidance in the following areas:

- Applicants Assisting Ethnocultural Communities, CPS-023
- Arts Activities and Charitable Registration, CG-018
- Benefits to Aboriginal Peoples of Canada, CPS-012
- Canadian Registered Charities Carrying Out Activities Outside Canada, CG-002
- Charitable Organizations Outside Canada that Have Received a Gift from Her Majesty in Right of Canada, CG-015
- Charitable Purposes and Activities that Benefit Youth, CG-020
- Charitable Work and Ethnocultural Groups - Information on registering as a charity, CG-003

- Community Economic Development Activities and Charitable Registration, CG-014
- Computers for Children, CPC-013
- Daycare Facilities, CPS-003
- Distinction Between Self-Help and Members' Groups, CPS-016
- Effective Date of Registration, CPS-017
- Festivals and the Promotion of Tourism, CPS-005
- Funding Qualified Donees, CPC-014
- Fundraising by Registered Charities, CG-013
- General Requirements for Charitable Registration, CG-017
- Group Insurance Rates for Registered Charities, CPC-022
- Guidelines for Registering a Charity - Meeting the Public Benefit Test, CPS-024
- Guidelines for the Registration of Umbrella Organizations and Title Holding Organizations, CPS-026
- Housing and Charitable Registration, CG-022
- Housing for Seniors (Life-Tenancy Agreement), CPC-004
- How to Draft Purposes for Charitable Registration, CG-019
- Political Activities, CPS-022
- Promotion of Animal Welfare and Charitable Registration, CG-011
- Promotion of Health and Charitable Registration, CG-021
- Promotion of Volunteerism, CPS-025
- Publishing a Magazine, CPC-027
- Registering Charities that Promote Racial Equality, CPS-021
- Registration of Arts Festivals, CPS-010
- Registration of Canadian Amateur Athletic Associations, CPS-011
- Relief of the Aged, CPS-002
- Research as a Charitable Activity, CPS-029
- School Councils, CPS-013
- Sports and Charitable Registration, CPS-027
- Upholding Human Rights and Charitable Registration, CG-001

Copies of all current policies are available at **www.runningacharity.ca**

PUBLIC BENEFIT

Public benefit has two components. First, assuming the charity was effective in pursuing its objects, would the result affect a significant segment of the public? Second, would that effect, in fact, be a benefit? Even where the intention is to restrict the activities to a minority in the population, certain groups have been found to have been a significant enough section of the population to satisfy the test. For example, most religious groups that qualify as a religion service a minority in most communities yet still satisfy the public benefit requirement. Other groups may have to prove to the CRA that the people who they wish to benefit, form a significant segment of the community in that area.

The benefit question also cannot be taken for granted. If the CRA does not have prior experience with the type of cause being undertaken, it may seek quantifiable evidence that there is a benefit to the public. The typical example of a situation where the benefit is questionable is where a charity undertakes to create a library in an area so remote it is virtually inaccessible. While clearly a library would be beneficial in an urban area, locating it in a remote rural area where nobody is actually expected to use the library, undermines the benefit.

The CRA may request measurable evidence of the benefit in question but quantifying benefit can be difficult for a potential organization. In fact, it may be impossible for an organization that has not yet undertaken activities and does not have the resources necessary to do sophisticated market research to prove that their approach meets the public benefit test. Generally, organizations with a novel approach to a community issue are advised to meet with experienced legal counsel prior to submitting their application for charitable status.

MODEL OBJECTS

Perhaps as a measure to increase their own efficiency, but also as a matter of concern for those organizations which seek charitable status, the Charities Directorate put out a list of objects for which they would approve the wording. These objects are known as the model objects and have been expanded once already. The model objects include charitable activities from all of the four different heads and should be reviewed by any organization seeking charitable status prior to submission of an application to the CRA. The current model objects are available in Appendix A. This list will be updated on **www.runningacharity.ca** as the Charities Directorate releases new objects.

DRAFTING OBJECTS

When reviewing the objects drafted by the organization, the CRA looks for three elements. The first element is the charitable category (i.e. the head of charity); the second element is the means of providing the charitable benefit, and the third is the eligible beneficiary group. This type of drafting is rather formulaic and may or may not be in the proposed charity's best interests. While drafting the objects in this manner is not (strictly speaking) necessary to qualify for charitable status, knowing that the Directorate pays special attention to such formulations does tend to help avoid a dispute with the CRA regarding the object's phrasing – if not the actual language.

The first element is often met by including the specific head of charity under which the charity intends to qualify. For example, "to advance education by . . . " or, "to relieve poverty by . . . " Where the object in question is in the general category of other activities, one would expect the wording to begin with the specific sub-category such as "to alleviate suffering and distress by . . . " or "to improve the aesthetic taste of the community by . . . "

The second element effectively refers to the primary activity or activities that the organization means to undertake to further its objects. For example, operating a food bank, or providing eye surgery. Prospective registrants should know that the information provided with respect to the activities will form the initial judgment of whether the organization is in fact charitable and whether it is formed for the public benefit.

The final element deals with the group of people who are the intended beneficiaries. This is rather self-explanatory but in terms of developing an object, would effectively circumscribe the people the organization can help. The organization may want to take an expansive view of this, not only because of the CRA's evaluation of the public benefit test, but also so that the organization has room to expand the group of people it wishes to help over time. An example of such a clause is the underlined portion of "to advance health by performing eye surgery for <u>the poor in El Salvador</u>" or to "relieve poverty by providing a soup kitchen for the <u>needy in Calgary</u>."

BROAD AND VAGUE

One of the CRA's most frequent objections to charitable purposes is that they are both overly broad and vague. Unfortunately, this accusation is hurled with such frequency that it seems clear that the original meaning of the term has been lost to the CRA. An overly broad object is one which allows the charitable organization to undertake non-charitable activities. Moreover, only objects can be overly broad, not activities.

A vague object is one in which it is impossible to tell what the organization intends to do. Broad and vague objects are dealt with in greater detail elsewhere in this book.

DESIGNATION

There are three types of registered charities in Canada: charitable organizations, public foundations and private foundations. Most organizations which intend to undertake activities to further their charitable objects are charitable organizations.

Foundations generally exist to give money to other qualified donees (mostly other registered charities). However, although there are some limitations on foundations which do not exist for charitable organizations, foundations can also undertake their own activities.

Charitable Organization

A charitable organization is effectively one which is not controlled by any single entity and which is organized to further its charitable objects through its own charitable activities.

Public Foundation

A public foundation is one where control is not exerted by any specific individual or group of individuals who are related to each other. As stated earlier, such organizations typically exist to provide funds to other qualified donees but may also decide to carry on their own activities.

Private Foundation

A private foundation is effectively one where control is exercised by a group of people related to each other. A private foundation is not limited to giving funds to other qualified donees and can undertake its own charitable activities as well, although this is not usually the case.

Internal CRA designation

The CRA maintains a list of categories in which it places every organization which it registers. This is not the same designation as a charitable organization or foundation as above. Rather, it is internal to the CRA and has no legal meaning at all. Organizations that fall into one category are just as much registered charitable organizations as those in another. For some reason, the CRA makes public the category under which it classifies an organization. At times this can become difficult for a group which wants to be registered under one category but is publicly recognized in another. This may happen in the example of an organization that believes itself to be religious (and at the lay sense might very well be) but which cannot be placed into that category because the law simply does not allow for it.

The evidence of the category in which a charity is placed may be found on the CRA's registered charity database under the definition of category. As there is no legal meaning to this designation it can safely be ignored until such time as the law gives some meaning to this categorization.

4

Registering as a Charity

THE T2050 FORM

The key to becoming registered as a charity in Canada is the Application for Registered Charity Status form submitted to the CRA. The technical CRA designation for this application is the T2050 Form. The form is updated from time to time and so it is important that the prospective charity use the form which is current as of the time of registration. In the past, the Charities Directorate has had some amount of grace for the old forms but as time goes by has ceased accepting old versions. The review in this chapter deals with the form T2050e11 - a copy of the current form is available at **www.runningacharity.ca**.

The Application for Registered Charity Status form will be examined from every angle by the Charities Directorate to determine whether the specific organization qualifies for registered charitable status. While the questions may seem innocuous, the CRA may use the form to take a strict view in registering potential charities. As a result, while the form is designed to be filled out by the layperson, the fact that the form will be compared against the body of charity law to determine whether the applicant will qualify means that there can be tremendous value in having an experienced charity law professional review the form if not fill it out completely.

The Charities Directorate has created a guide for use by lay people to completing the T2050 form. That guide is called the T4063. The guide is an adequate explanation of the information that the Charities Directorate reviews but it does not explain why the information is being sought, so that individuals filling out the form can have some sense of the legal ramifications of their answers. With some understanding of the reason the information being sought, prospective charities can answer more fully and forcefully. At times, we have seen tremendous misunderstandings arise because of approaches taken by different groups in completing the form. This may happen, for example, where a group's religious beliefs are listed in a foreign language or the religious activities, at least superficially, are not put in a religious context.

As the guide is adequate for filling out the form, this chapter will provide additional commentary without repeating the information in the guide (available at **www.runningacharity.ca**). This will hopefully assist those trying to fill out the application for charitable status on their own, and provide the information that the CRA is looking for in proper context. This will improve the prospective charity's chances for charitable registration.

Part 1: Identification of the Organization

As discussed previously, an organization must be organized as an entity before it can apply for charitable registration. This section of the form seeks to identify the organization making the application.

An organization that was previously registered as a charity but lost its registration would also indicate so here. For the sake of clarity, a new organization will have a current name but will not have a previous name or a business number. On the other hand, an organization that has been operating for some time should have a business name and may have previous names by which it was known. It may also have previous contact with the CRA and/or may be applying for re-registration as a charity.

It should be understood that all organizations will be judged on the record that is presented to the CRA and on information gleaned from internal resources and the internet. The CRA applies the charity law regime rules to organizations that are seeking registered charity status even though they were not subject to such rules prior to registration. It is therefore easy to understand why a brand new organization may have a better chance at registration than an organization that has been operating for some time. A new organization simply has a cleaner record and less chance that it has fallen offside.

An older organization will have a more difficult time obtaining registered charity status as will organizations that have already been revoked for cause. Indeed even some organizations that were revoked for failure to file will also find it impossible to be reregistered as a charity. In these cases, the CRA may be using the organizations' previous history as a means to deny registration. Of course, the organization may appeal this decision through the process described in Chapter 7.

At times we have seen situations where prospective charities have applied on their own to the Charities Directorate for registered charity status. The Application was rejected, usually for good reason, because the Applicant did not properly understand the obligations of a charity and the registration system. Applying again, the organization runs the risk of having its past record being applied against it even if the organization manages to clean up its act. It simply may be that the Charities Directorate does not believe that the new organization with its new *modus operandi* is substantially different to the one which failed at registration.

In circumstances like this, some groups may abandon the old organization and start afresh with a new organization and a clean record so that there is little confusion as to what this new organization will attempt to accomplish. Again, it is important that the application is complete and truthful but it is also true that by applying with a clean slate, the organization stands a better chance at being registered as a charity.

The timelines for considering applications vary depending on the backlog at the Charities Directorate and the staffing situation at the time the application is submitted. In our experience it takes between six and nine months for an application to be considered and taken to its final determination. There are no firm time commitments from the CRA on processing an application. The Charities Directorate will expedite an application if it can be shown that the organization is expecting a large donation or has a significant fundraising event coming up. Furthermore, where it is a matter of life and death (such as after a disaster) the CRA may well expedite the application so the charity can begin its work. Of course, this does not mean it will register an organization that does not deserve to qualify, and so it is still important that the applicant make every effort to structure its affairs in a way which complies with the law and with which the CRA will agree.

The registered office address of the entity is the address at which its books and records will officially be kept. This address will go on file and the CRA will expect that this requirement be followed.

Finally, Part I of the form requests the charity's website and email address. If the charity does not have these in place, it is not compelled to acquire them in order that the CRA may have them.

It is important to note that the CRA will check the charity's website for evidence that the applicant qualifies for charitable registration. In addition, the CRA will do a Google search of the charity's name and even its directors. Again, while an applicant is not a "charity" and is not subject to the charity rules, the CRA may use whatever it finds on the internet as evidence of the proposition that the organization would not have qualified if the laws applied to them. For this reason it is important that the organization review its online content prior to submitting an application. The review should take into account any factors which the CRA may misunderstand as activities which the organization would inappropriately carry on *after* being granted charitable registration status. Also, the organization may wish to make clear any relationships with similar organizations in other countries.

Part 2: Organizational structure

In the previous chapter, we discussed the different ways in which a corporation can be organized. In Part 2 of the T2050, the organization provides the necessary information for the Charities Directorate files.

The first question this section asks is whether or not the organization forms the internal division of another organization. Generally speaking, where an organization has its own governing documents it will not form a subdivision of another organization. This is also true where there exists an umbrella organization and the applicant has sister organizations all with their own incorporating documents.

Where an applicant *is* part of the internal division of another registered charity, the Charities Directorate will require a letter of good standing from the parent organization.

To complete the application for charitable status the organization must include a copy of its governing documents. This may also include a constitution or memorandum of association, trust document or (depending on the jurisdiction of the incorporation) letters patent, articles of incorporation. In addition, if the organization has bylaws and minutes it would be required to also forward them.

At times, an organization may register as an unincorporated association and then later incorporate. While we generally discourage organizations from operating in such a way, there are several advantages to registering as an unincorporated organization first. The primary advantage is the cost. It costs very little to set up an unincorporated association and should the applicant fail to achieve registered charity status it can easily unwind such an organization. Furthermore, should the Charities Directorate request any changes to the governing documents it is a simple matter to amend the governing documents of an unincorporated association. (Conversely an incorporated entity may require significant documentation and in the case of an Alberta company, a court order to amend objects.)

Where the group proceeds in this manner and the Charities Directorate grants registered charity status to an association, the next step is to incorporate a new corporation with the exact same objects as the previous one. The group would then advise the CRA that it has begun carrying out operations as a corporation. The CRA would then transfer the status and issue a new registered charity number to the organization.

Part 3: Activities of the organization

This part of the application for charitable status is probably the single most important part of the application. It should be completed with deliberation and caution as the Charities Directorate will scour the activities for any indication that the applicant does not qualify.

i. Statement of activities

There is no such thing as "charitable activities." Activities cannot be characterized as being charitable or not charitable in and of themselves. The question which must be answered is whether the particular activities further the organization's objects. Of course, that is not to say that any activity which furthers a particular object is necessarily acceptable, but neither is it to say that a particular activity can be judged to disqualify the organization because it doesn't *sound* like something a charity should be doing.

The question that the Charities Directorate must answer is whether the activities further the charitable objects or whether they indicate that the organization has an unstated purpose (particularly a non-charitable one). Of course the additional test is whether the activities somehow put the charity offside the rules of the *Income Tax Act* or potentially one of the other federal statutes. The T2050 form requests that each activity be listed under the particular charitable object. This is a nod to the Charities Directorate's obligation to determine whether the particular activity is in furtherance of that specific object.

When describing the activities, keep in mind that the Charities Directorate is looking for evidence of what the charity is doing, how it is doing it and for whom it is doing it. It is important that the explanation be specific and clear. It is also important to remember that the officers of the Charities Directorate are not necessarily experts in the particular area in which the charity will operate. For example, we have dealt with charitable applications on behalf of groups who wish to relieve poverty in distant parts of the world using new technology. The use and applicability of this technology could not reasonably be expected to be known to the charity examiner. It therefore becomes important to explain the nature of the activity and how it furthers the organization's charitable objects.

The application process is hindered by the seemingly endless turnover of staff at the Directorate examiner level. Over time one would expect a certain charity examiner to become familiar with, for example, the intricacies of the charities working to preserve the environment. As the turnover is so great, it often happens that just as examiners achieve a level of comfort they leave the charities examiner role at the CRA.

The applicant must also remember that the Directorate can do their own research. In these circumstances, the Directorate's examiner will use the internet to dig up additional information on the organization. This often results in confusion because the information on the website is intended for one audience (usually donors) and not contextualized for the CRA. At times, the Directorate's examiner will raise true and critical reasons why the organization does not deserve charitable registration based on the content of the website. We commented earlier in this chapter that it is important that the organization review its online content prior to charitable registration and we reiterate that it is critical that the website reflect the organization's commitment to operating in accordance with charity law.

As Canada is a country of immigrants, many people start organizations to operate in their home country. When applicants include on the form that the organization will be operating outside the country, the Directorate will look for the proper legal means by which it can engage in such activities. The Directorate has published guidance on the point called "Operating with Foreign Intermediaries."

The most common way of operating with a foreign intermediary is through the use of an agency agreement. The law of agency is ancient and complicated. Organizations that will be operating with an agent should seek legal advice about the liabilities that might arise. An example of an agency agreement has been included at **www.runningacharity.ca**. A sample form should be reviewed and amended if necessary but keep in mind that many charities in this country have lost their charitable status for failing to meet the detailed requirements of an agency agreement.

ii. Fundraising activities

From the mid-1990's straight through the 2000's the Charities Directorate had as its mission to shut down a variety of tax shelters which they found offensive. As all of these tax shelters involved (in one form or another) donations to charity, the Directorate decided to use the T2050 form as a way to identify charities which may be engaging with tax shelters. It does this by asking specific questions related to fundraising. These questions have the additional benefit (from the Directorate's perspective) of identifying whether an organization is involved in any kind of an unrelated business or simply spending too much money on fundraising activity. While fundraising expenses are a concern for many Canadians and the Charities Directorate takes the position that certain levels of fundraising expenses are inappropriate, the fact remains that regulating fundraising expenses is beyond the jurisdiction of the Charities Directorate. Nevertheless, if the Directorate finds that these expenses are too high it will find some reason to justify denying registration (or revoking the organization's charitable status).

Most organizations have little to fear from questions of fundraising expenses. Similarly most organizations that involve the solicitation of donations by volunteers will not concern the Charities Directorate. Organizations that may be involved in business activities to raise funds for their organization should see Chapter 6 of this book.

iii. Political activities

Charities cannot engage in partisan political activities. This means that any charity that is campaigning for, or in support of (either vocally or through its resources in any way) either a specific candidate or a political party is subject to revocation of its charitable status or denial of registration. Any organization intending to engage in such activities should not bother registering in the first place. On the other hand, political activity which is related to the organizations charitable objects and where that activity occupies less than 10% of the organizations resources (it is an open question how that is calculated and it includes financial capital and volunteer resources) can be registered. The question in the T2050 form is designed to try and elicit that sort of information.

Financial information

The financial information section of the T2050 form is mostly an exercise in fantasy. Most organizations believe that they are going to raise vast sums for their charitable mission. Undoubtedly this estimation is based on their understanding of the perceived importance of their cause and the assumption that others will agree with them about this importance. However, this ignores the business realities of raising money. In our conversations with the Charities Directorate it is clear that most officers also recognize the futility of seeking realistic estimations from prospective charities. For this reason it is a wonder that the Directorate still continues to ask for this information. Nevertheless, the application form is certified by an officer of the organization and for that reason (if for no other) the form must be filled out truthfully and as realistically as possible.

i. Proposed budget

Two key elements to keep in mind when completing the proposed budget is (a) to make sure it is internally consistent and (b) that it considers the ratios of fundraising to spending.

Internal consistency refers to the requirement that the numbers have some logic between them. For example, if the organization claims it will only be operating domestically and it reports spending funds abroad, the Directorate will come to the understanding that it is operating there as well.

Similarly, while the Directorate will likely take the numbers in a proposed budget with a grain of salt, it will look at the various ratios to see if the charity is in line with the Directorate's expectations. For example, if the organization intends to spend over 35% of its revenue on fundraising, the Directorate will then question whether or not this is appropriate and whether the organization exists to further charitable objects or simply to fundraise (which is not charitable).

Information about officials

While this section may seem relatively innocuous in that the questions simply asks for information about the directors or trustees of the organization, there are certain things to keep in mind.

First, all the information is required. If a birthdate is missing, the Charities Directorate will return the entire application to you (generally after a one-month delay) telling you that they need the information. You will then have to seek this information, include it in the form and return the package to the Directorate where it will be returned to the end of the queue.

Second, the information that is included in the form will be used by the CRA for its various purposes. For example, if a director was the director of another charity that has been revoked for cause the new organization may not qualify for charitable registration. The Directorate maintains a list of individuals who are ineligible to serve as directors and will contact you if one of these individuals appears on the new charity roster. Similarly, the Directorate may cross-reference the list of names with other lists that it maintains and return to you with questions or concerns.

Confidential information

The term "confidential" is awkward given that all the information the form requests would seem to be confidential. The reason it is considered confidential is that the rest of the form may become available to the public. For reasons of security and some degree of privacy, the Directorate agrees to keep certain information confidential.

Certification

The application form must be signed prior to submission. It should be signed by two directors of the organization with knowledge about the applicant's affairs. Directors who are certifying the form should take it seriously, even if there is no real possibility of punishment for errors made.

POST-APPLICATION PROCESS

Once the application form is submitted to the Charities Directorate it will be reviewed first by a front-line person to determine that the application is complete. If so, the CRA confirms that the application is complete it will be assigned a file number. A letter indicating the file number will be forwarded to the applicant's contact person or authorized representative. Then, depending on the backlog at the CRA, the application will be viewed by the examiner and a decision will be made about its treatment. The usual options in this case are to register the applicant as a charity or to respond with a letter requesting further information about the applicant. In some circumstances, the Directorate will agree to register the organization if certain changes are made in the applicant's objects or governing documents.

Assuming all the requirements are met, the notification of registration will be sent to the organization and it may begin its charitable operations with its business number included on that paper.

If the organization receives a "Notice of Refusal of Registration" it may begin the dispute process resolution described in Chapter 7.

PART II

Maintaining a Charity

5

Raising Funds

Convincing a donor to make a gift to a charity is partly an appeal to the individual's sense of altruism and partly a practical discussion of the cost of the gift to the donor. Therefore, in order to effectively solicit a donation, the prospective donee must have a good working knowledge of the cost of the donation to the donor - the object, of course, being to maximize the size of the donation and minimize its cost. To paraphrase Jean-Baptiste Colbert in his famous statement about taxation, the art of fundraising consists in so plucking the goose as to get the most feathers with the least hissing. Since donations to registered charities are given a special tax treatment, the actual cost to the donor must be determined with reference to the *Income Tax Act* (ITA or Act). Unfortunately, the ITA is a huge, unwieldy and extremely technical document not designed for casual reference. To make matters worse, the after-tax cost to the donor may depend on the item donated (and in some cases, on who is the recipient of the gift). This chapter is designed to give readers an understanding of the after-tax cost of donations to donors, as a means to improve fundraising efforts and ultimately increase the amount of donations coming into the organization.

While chapter one discusses the basic tax concepts necessary to understand some of the more complex issues in this chapter, a small review is worthwhile. Canada has a progressive income tax structure. This means that as income rises, so does the tax rate on the next dollar. For example, all other things being equal, everyone would pay the same tax on their first $35,000 of taxable income. Those who earn more than $35,000 would pay a higher rate on their next $35,000 of taxable income (or any portion thereof), and so on. When income is earned in a year, it is generally taxable. So, if an individual receives $1,000 from her employer, she is taxed on $1,000.

Similarly, there are tax consequences if an individual sells or donates a piece of property. If the item is inventory in a business for that individual, the profits of the sale or donation are considered income and treated in the same manner as if they had been paid by an employer. On the other hand, if the donor owns the property to earn income from it, but not through the sale of it, it is generally considered a piece of capital property.

Example:

An individual with a stock portfolio who does not engage in heavy trading likely owns the shares as *capital property,* whereas an individual who earns his or her daily living by trading shares likely holds them as *inventory*. When a piece of capital property is eventually sold, the owner is generally taxed on the gain in value that occurred while he or she owned that particular item. This is called a capital gain, and only 50% of it is taxable. If a capital item decreases in value while held by the owner, it is a capital loss and is not taxable.

The tax consequence of a sale or gift (called a disposition) is the single biggest factor affecting the cost of a donation. Thus, a familiarity with these rules is crucial to raising significant donations.

Donation of Income vs. Capital

	Income	Capital
Amount of donation	$1,000	$1,000
Taxable amount	$1,000	$500
Tax rate	46%	46%
Tax owing	$460	$230

After the amount of tax owing is calculated, tax credits are subtracted from this amount to determine the total amount payable. Notably, if nothing is owing, tax credits do not result in a payment to the taxpayer. Donations by individuals result in tax credits. The tax credit itself is determined by multiplying the first $200 by the lowest combined federal/provincial rate in the appropriate province (except Alberta, ON and BC), and multiplying everything over $200 by the highest rate.[4] The following table illustrates the tax credits available for donations of $1,200 in the different provinces.

4 The exception to this rule exists at the new income tax rates of over $514,090 in Ontario where the tax credit does not match the tax one pays.

Donations on $1,200 in donations for 2014

Province	Tax credit rate on first $200 donation	Tax Credit	Tax credit rate on next $1000 of donations	Tax credit on next $1000 donation	Total combined Federal and Provincial tax credit
Alberta	25.00%	$ 50.00	50.00%	$500.00	$ 550.00
British Columbia	20.06%	$ 40.12	43.70%	$437.00	$ 477.12
Manitoba	25.8%	$ 51.60	46.40%	$464.00	$ 515.60
New Brunswick	24.68%	$ 49.36	46.84%	$468.40	$ 517.76
Newfoundland	22.70%	$ 45.40	42.30%	$423.00	$ 468.40
Northwest Territories	20.90%	$ 41.80	43.05%	$430.50	$ 472.30
Nova Scotia	23.79%	$ 47.58	50.00%	$500.00	$ 547.58
Nunavut	19.00%	$ 38.00	40.50%	$405.00	$ 443.00
Ontario[5]	20.05%	$ 40.10	40.16%	$401.60	$ 441.70
Prince Edward Island[6]	24.80%	$ 49.60	45.70%	$457.00	$ 506.60
Saskatchewan	26.00%	$ 52.00	44.00%	$440.00	$ 492.00
Yukon	22.04%	$ 44.08	41.76%	$417.60	$ 461.68

To simplify the discussion, this chapter will make several assumptions. First, unless otherwise stated, the donor holds the items to be donated as capital property. Second, we will assume a credit rate of 46%.

DONATIONS OF CASH

Donations of cash are fairly straightforward. The charity simply receipts the face value of the amount donated. (This does not apply to currency held for collection purposes). Assuming that the donor earned that cash in the same year it was donated, then tax would otherwise have to be paid on it (ignoring for a moment the practical issue that taxes on employment income are generally deducted at the source). If the donor is in the highest income tax bracket, the tax credits generated from the donation would offset the tax owing on the income earned and so no tax would be payable on the money earned – and then donated. At lower income brackets, and in Alberta, the credits would actually more than offset the tax owing and the donor would be able to shelter other income from tax with the credits earned from this donation, assuming the donation is greater than $200. Similarly, if the donor is donating cash that is not income to him in the year donating, the credit could be used to offset taxes owing from other sources.

FIRST TIME DONOR'S CREDIT

The *First Time Donor's Credit* (FTDC) was instituted for a five-year trial period in the 2013 Federal Budget. As the name would suggest, it is a special tax credit for those who have not donated to charity before. However, because of the technical application of the credit, it applies if neither the taxpayer nor their spouse has claimed a donation tax credit since 2007.

The FTDC increases the value of the federal portion of the donations tax credit by 25 percentage points on the first $1,000 in cash donations claimed in respect of any one taxation year from 2013 to 2017.

So whereas the federal credit on the first $200 of donations is normally $30 (15%), for those claiming the FTDC it is $80 (40%); and for the amount between $200 and $1000 the amount is normally $282 (29%) but under the FTDC is $ 432 (54%).

The enhanced credit is only available in the first year a donor or spouse (including common law) claim it and even if claimed for only $20, the credit will no longer be available for the remaining $980.

PUBLIC SECURITIES

As discussed, Canada has a capital gains tax that is levied on 50% of the *appreciation in value* of the capital good. The tax is levied when the item is disposed of (i.e. sold or given away). Under most circumstances, it is irrelevant whether the asset is sold or donated. However, the ITA does contain an exemption for certain capital assets donated to a registered charity such as publicly listed securities donated to charity (note that this does not include shares held in an RRSP, RRIF, or pension plan). The exemption means that no tax is payable when public securities are donated to a registered charity. Moreover, the donor continues to receive a donation tax receipt equal to the fair market value of the shares donated. Thus, there is no tax on the donation, but the donor still receives a tax credit equal to the fair market value of the donation.

A publicly listed security is effectively any share listed on a number of exchanges throughout the world. This list of exchanges is defined by regulation and changes from time to time. As of January 2014 the list includes:

- Canada: Canadian National Stock Exchange (CNSX); Montreal Exchange; TSX Venture Exchange (Tiers 1 and 2); Toronto Stock Exchange
- Australia: Australian Securities Exchange
- Austria: Vienna Stock Exchange
- Belgium: Euronext Brussels
- Bermuda: Bermuda Stock Exchange
- Czech Republic: Prague Stock Exchange (Prime Market)
- Denmark: Copenhagen Stock Exchange
- Finland: Helsinki Stock Exchange
- France: Euronext Paris
- Germany: Frankfurt Stock Exchange; Boerse Stuttgart AG (Stuttgart Stock Exchange)
- Hong Kong: The Hong Kong Stock Exchange
- Ireland: Irish Stock Exchange
- Israel: Tel Aviv Stock Exchange
- Italy: Milan Stock Exchange
- Japan: Tokyo Stock Exchange
- Luxembourg: Luxembourg Stock Exchange
- Mexico: Mexico City Stock Exchange
- Netherlands: Euronext Amsterdam
- New Zealand: New Zealand Stock Exchange
- Norway: Oslo Stock Exchange
- Poland: The main and parallel markets of the Warsaw Stock Exchange
- Singapore: Singapore Stock Exchange
- South Africa: Johannesburg Stock Exchange
- Spain: Madrid Stock Exchange
- Sweden: Stockholm Stock Exchange
- Switzerland: SWX Swiss Exchange
- United Kingdom: London Stock Exchange
- United States: Boston Stock Exchange; Chicago Board of Options; Chicago Board of Trade; Chicago Stock Exchange; National Association of Securities Dealers Automated Quotation System (NASDAQ); National Stock Exchange; New York Stock Exchange; NYSE Arca; NYSE MKT; Philadelphia Stock Exchange.

Example:

Assume that Nell lives in Ontario and buys one share of a high-tech company for $1.00. Over time, the share rises in value and may even split once or more than once. After ten years, with all splits factored in, Nell owns shares worth a total of $100. If Nell were to sell the share she would have a capital gain of $99 (i.e. the fair market value of $100, less the cost of $1). Applying the capital gains inclusion rate of 50%, only $47.50 would be taxable. Further applying a tax rate of 46% the amount of tax payable would be $21.85. Thus, if Nell sells the shares she is left with after-tax income of $78.15 (i.e. $100 - $21.85).

Conversely, let's say Nell decides she wants to donate her shares instead of selling them. In this case, Nell has no tax to pay and of course, receives no income from the sale of the share. She does however receive a tax receipt for $100, which will offset $46 of taxes due from other sources. So, assuming Nell is paying tax on income from other sources, the actual after-tax cost of this donation is $54.

FLOW-THROUGH SHARES

Flow-through shares are defined in extremely technical language in the *Income Tax Act*, but are fairly easy to understand. Generally speaking, the ITA imposes tax on the amount of income earned by a taxpayer, less any amounts deducted. Expenses incurred to earn income are deductible. However, one can only deduct these expenses from income earned; if no income is earned, the deductions are lost.

Mining companies incur significant expenses before they create a revenue stream. So, in order to encourage investment in the mining sector, the federal government basically allows the owner of a flow-through share to deduct expenses incurred by the mining company from his or her personal income. To make things even better, the federal government has provided a "super flow-through" credit of 15%, which it tends to renew in each federal budget.

The catch is that, for income tax purposes, the cost of the share is deemed to be zero. So even if the buyer buys the share at $10.00 and sells it at $8.00, the share is still assumed to have gained $8.00 in value and is therefore taxed on an $8.00 capital gain even though it actually lost $2.00. Of course, given that the shareholder will have already deducted the purchase price of the share from his or her income, and capital gains are only taxed at half the amount of other income, the incentive still exists to buy the share. Generally speaking, it is unlikely that a donor will be willing to donate a flow-through share prior to receiving the deduction of expenses. However, regardless of whether the deductions are used by the donor, they are useless to the charity.

Example:

Assuming the deductions from the shares are already used by the donor, imagine a situation where Elana bought publicly traded shares for $5,000 and they are now worth $6,000. She can either sell them for $6,000 or donate them to a charity for $6,000. As the cost of these shares is deemed to be $0, if she sells them there will be a capital gain of $6000 (and a taxable capital gain of $3,000). At a tax rate of 46% she will have a tax liability of $1,380. So ignoring the value of the deduction, Elana must pay $1,380 of tax on a gain of $1,000.

On the other hand, when donated to charity, there is no tax on the increase in value greater than the purchase price. So, if these publicly traded shares are donated to charity, Elana will pay capital gains tax on the purchase price of $5000 and receive a tax receipt for $6,000, which will offset approximately $2,760 of taxes including $1,150 from this transaction ($5000 being the deemed capital gain, only half of which is taxable multiplied by a 46% tax rate).

Purchase price	FMV of donation	Tax payable	Tax value of receipt	Credits remaining to offset other taxes
$5,000	$4,000	$920	$1,840	$920
$5,000	$5,000	$1,150	$2,300	$1,150
$5,000	$6,000	$1,150	$2,760	$1,610

Of course, when working with a particular donor, it may be in the charity's interest to have the donor purchase flow-through shares with the intention of donating them after the deductions are taken. In these cases, the charity should consult with an accountant to calculate the value of the relevant deductions in the donor's province of residence.

STOCK OPTIONS

Most businesses are organized as corporations, with ownership of the corporation divided into shares. Shareholders are entitled to, among other things, a share of the profits of the corporation. Shares of many corporations can be bought and sold on stock exchanges around the world. The price of these shares is based on a perception of the value of the company. As an incentive to employees to help increase the value of the company, corporations often offer employees the right to purchase shares of the corporation for a lower price than they are traded at on the stock exchanges.

Generally, the price at which employees can purchase the shares (the "strike price") is a set price. Assuming the employee exercises the option at a point when the fair market value of the share (i.e. market price) is greater than the strike price, the employee will pay tax on the difference between them.

Assuming the shares are publicly listed, if the employee exercises the option to purchase and donates them to charity within 30 days, there will be no tax payable on the disposition and the donor will receive a tax credit for the full amount of the donation. If, on the other hand, the donor donates the options themselves, he or she will not be entitled to a receipt until the charity exercises the option – if ever. For more information, see the section earlier in this chapter on the donation of public securities.

DERIVATIVES

While shares of publicly-traded corporations are the most popular form of security to be donated to charity, there are a variety of other sophisticated financial securities that may also be donated. Examples include: exchange-traded funds, index funds, hedge funds, warrants, rights, and put and call options. As long as these products qualify as publicly-traded securities, they will qualify for the special tax treatment accorded donations of this type.

PRIVATE SECURITIES

Despite the omnipresence of the CRA, Canada's income tax system is essentially self-administered. As a result, temptation abounds to conduct business with non-arm's length people (including oneself) in order to ensure a tax result that would not have occurred were all parties strangers to one another. Therefore, the ITA contains a variety of provisions designed to prevent taxpayers from surrendering to temptation.

One situation where a donor may be left in the position of too much control over a gift involves the donation of securities in a private corporation to a foundation controlled by the donor. The problem is easy to see; if one can donate securities of a corporation controlled by the donor to a charity controlled by the donor, the donor will be in a position to create a never-ending stream of tax receipts for which the foundation might not see any benefit.

Unfortunately, the ITA provisions to prevent this situation are drafted so broadly that they also affect donations to charities other than private foundations. Essentially, the donation of securities of private corporations is dealt with in one of two ways; either the gifts are "excepted," or they are not. An excepted gift is a share donated to a charitable organization or public foundation where the donor deals at arm's length with the charity, its directors/trustees, officers, and other like officials. Thus, a donor wishing to donate shares of a private company has an incentive to give them to a charity where he or she does not have any close relations serving in any capacity with the charity, and a disincentive to give them to a charity in which a close relation is serving in any capacity. In these latter circumstances, the gift is no longer an "excepted gift" and the rules for a "non-qualifying" security apply.

In cases where the gift has been donated to a private foundation or to a public charity to which the donor is related, the gift is not considered "made" until one of two things happen: either the item donated must cease to be a non-qualifying security (e.g. the corporation is no longer controlled by the donor, or the corporation becomes publicly listed), or the charity must dispose of the security within five years of receiving the donation. The fair market value of the gift is then the lesser of:

a. the value of the security when transferred to the charity, and
b. the value of the security when the gift is deemed to have been made (ie. the shares are sold).

Example:

Imagine that Naomi and Isaac own a very successful snack food business that they started from scratch. As a good community citizen, Isaac serves as a director of a public foundation in support of the local university. Seeing Isaac's commitment to this cause, Naomi wants to donate some of her shares in their business, worth $150,000, to the public foundation. If Naomi does this, the gift is not considered made until Isaac is either no longer involved with the foundation, or the foundation disposes of the shares (within five years of the gift having been made).

Let us further assume that three years later Isaac is still a director of the foundation and the business buys back the donated shares from the foundation for $100,000. Given that Naomi and Isaac started the business from scratch, to them the cost of the shares is likely negligible. They therefore have a capital gain in the year in which the charity sold the shares of the lesser of the value of the shares when donated ($150,000) and when sold ($100,000). (Because these shares are not publicly traded they do not qualify for the tax- free exemption discussed earlier). However, the taxation of these shares only occurs at half the rate it would have been if they had not been donated to a charity at all. Thus, of the $100,000, only 50% is taxable. On this $50,000, we apply our assumed tax rate of 46% to arrive at tax owing of $23,000. Naomi is still entitled to a tax receipt for $100,000, and would have tax credits totalling $46,000, more than offsetting the tax owing.

It is important to note that the donor does not have to include any capital gain in their income before the shares are sold by the charity, so that the donor is not paying tax in advance of receiving the receipt. If the charity does not sell the shares within five years, the donor will not receive a receipt and the gain will never be taxable.

RRSPS/RRIFS

A Registered Retirement Savings Plan (RRSP) is a type of financial umbrella that allows deposits to accumulate tax-free until they are withdrawn from under the umbrella. In the year in which money is contributed to an RRSP (i.e. put under the umbrella) it is deductible from the income of the contributor. Only certain types of assets can be deposited into an RRSP, but fortunately the list is quite long and includes cash, securities, and even gold bullion. Once in an RRSP, deposits can be converted from one form to another without any tax consequences. While the ITA allows income to accumulate in an RRSP tax-free, it does not allow an RRSP to exist forever. By the age of 71, one's RRSP must be converted into a *Registered Retirement Income Fund* (RRIF).

Money placed in an RRSP is not inaccessible to the owner of the RRSP; it can be withdrawn at any time, but is taxable then. (Notably, there are exceptions for first-time home buyers and for those engaged in lifelong learning programs). Given the strong incentive to contribute to an RRSP, many Canadians involved in tax planning try to maximize their contributions, with the consequence that they do not have much income leftover to make large charitable contributions.

That said, people may find that they have more than enough money in their RRSPs once they get to a certain age, and are willing to make donations in their lifetime in order to see the fruits of those donations while they are still alive. The RRSP rules do allow for withdrawals from the plan, but upon withdrawal the institution that holds the account (usually a bank) is required to withhold certain amounts. These amounts, on a per withdrawal basis (i.e. not cumulatively for the year), are:

- 10% (21% in Québec) on withdrawals up to $5,000
- 20% (26% in Québec) on withdrawals between $5,001 - $15,000
- 30% (31% in Québec) on withdrawals of more than $15,000.

The amounts withdrawn are claimed as income to the owner of the RRSP in the year withdrawn and tax is paid at the owner's marginal rate. Thus, if a potential donor wants to make a donation of $50,000 and has that money under the RRSP umbrella, a withdrawal of $50,000 would give the potential donor outside of Québec $35,000 cash to donate. The remaining thirty percent ($15,000 in this case) would be remitted to the government by the bank and credited as income tax already paid when the donor files his tax returns for that year.

A donor may also wish to donate his or her RRSP or RRIF upon death. There are two ways to do this. One way is to list the charity as a beneficiary of the RRSP in the donor's Will. The other way is to make use of the direct beneficiary election, which is signed when the RRSP is first opened (and can usually be changed at will). If the first method is used, the RRSP will fall into the donor's general estate before passing on to the charity. Under the second method, the RRSP will automatically become the property of the charity without going through the estate. The advantage of using the RRSP direct beneficiary election is that the RRSP will not pass through probate. When a Will is probated, the various provinces charge different amounts of tax on the total value of assets passed on in the Will. Thus, the amount of money in an RRSP is added to the other assets and a portion is taken by the government before any of the assets are passed on. In Ontario, these taxes are 0.5% on the first $50,000 of value in the estate and 1.5% on all amounts over $50,000. [5]

Also, probating a Will takes time and the charity might not be interested in waiting for that process to wend its way through the courts, particularly if the Will is being challenged by the other beneficiaries.

In the year of death, a taxpayer is entitled to offset one hundred percent of the tax owed by making donations. As one hundred percent of the RRSP income would otherwise be included as taxable income in the year of death, donating that amount to a charity would offset this income completely. It would also make use of the unlimited tax credit rule in the year of death.

5 This is not as big of an issue in every province and so it should be evaluated accordingly.

INSURANCE

Anything that constitutes property can be transferred to another person. This includes contracts of insurance. For the most part, insurance has been overlooked by charities as a method of raising funds, but it is important for charities to be flexible in their thinking when sourcing donations. They may be able to amass donations of items they would otherwise never have sought, let alone receive. One such area that deserves further focus by charities is life insurance.

Life insurance is a product that is bought to plan for specific situations. In some cases, it is to provide for one's family at the death of the primary earner in a family, or to pay costs arising on death. However, life insurance also plays an important part in business arrangements, such as being collateral for a loan or providing funds for certain share purchase arrangements. No matter the reason that life insurance was purchased, it is always possible that the reason will cease to exist. For example, a business loan may have been repaid, or children in a family may have become financially independent. When the original reason for purchasing the policy disappears, the costs of the policy become unnecessary. By providing a place for the owners of superfluous policies to dispose of them, charities may realize significant revenue while playing a useful role in the economy.

From a tax perspective, the donor will have an income inclusion of the proceeds of disposition less the *adjusted cost base* (ACB). An income inclusion is distinct from a capital gain and effectively means that a donation of an insurance policy has no net tax benefit for the donor. The ACB calculation is rather complicated and takes into account the premiums paid, dividends received, and (for policies purchased after 1982) the *Net Cost of Pure Insurance* (NCPI). Despite the ominous name, the NCPI is not overly difficult to calculate, although it will likely require professional advice from either an experienced advisor or the insurance company involved.

In a February 2008 bulletin, and later in another setting, the CRA laid down certain guidelines for determining the FMV of a disposed-of policy. In these pronouncements, the *proceeds of disposition* (POD) of an insurance policy takes into account:

- the policy's loan value;
- the face value of the policy;
- the state of health of the insured and his/her life expectancy;
- conversion privileges;
- other policy terms, such as term riders, double indemnity provisions; and
- replacement value.

The idea here is that the value of a policy may or may not be accurately reflected by any cash surrender value held by the policy. When valuing the policy for both tax and receipting purposes, the donor and the charity must take into account the fact that the donor may be very ill and the policy may mature shortly after donation. A policy that would otherwise be impossible to receipt would become valuable to the donor. Unfortunately, the advice of an actuary and an appraiser is critical to correctly valuing the insurance policy.

The charity may either cash the policy and use the funds immediately, or pay the premiums on the policy and collect the larger death benefit when the insured dies. Of course, a very generous donor may not only donate the policy to the charity but donate the yearly premiums to the charity as well. In this case both the donation of the policy and the donated premiums would be receiptable.

ANNUITIES

An annuity is a contract under which one person deposits a sum of money with another in exchange for a subsequent income. It is basically the reverse concept of insurance. The income may be paid for either a specified period, for life, or for life with a minimum guaranteed period. Under the latter method, if the purchaser of the annuity dies during the guaranteed period, the annuity will be paid to some other person whom the purchaser had designated to receive it.

Although annuities are normally purchased from insurance companies or trust companies, life annuities are sometimes purchased from charities. Essentially, a person gives the charity a sum of money irrevocably in exchange for a promise by the charity to pay the donor a monthly income for life. The funds received would then be invested by the charity at a higher rate than it would pay to the donor.

Annuity payments are usually a blend of capital return and interest. Changes to the ITA result in different treatments for annuities made before and after December 21, 2002. For annuities issued before that date, only the interest portion is taxable. This interest may, however, be eligible for either the *interest income deduction or the pension income deduction* provided by the ITA. For annuities issued after December 21, 2002, the donor would be eligible to receive a receipt for an amount equal to the excess of the amount contributed by the donor over the amount that would be paid at that time to an arm's-length third party to acquire an annuity to fund the guaranteed payments.

Example:

If an individual were to donate $100,000 to a charity and receive annual payments in return, and the charity purchased a $50,000 annuity to fund the payments, under the new rules the donor would be entitled to a receipt for $50,000. If the annuity payments and the value of the receipt are greater than the amount actually donated, the excess will be included in income as the payments are received by the donor.

ARTWORK

The donation of artwork in Canada falls into two broad categories based on whether or not the artwork is certified *Canadian Cultural Property* and donated to a designated institution. Artwork that qualifies as *Canadian Cultural Property* is dealt with in the next section. Artwork which is *not* certified as Canadian cultural property qualifies as *Listed Personal Property* discussed later in this chapter.

CANADIAN CULTURAL PROPERTY

The Canadian government has set up the *Canadian Cultural Property Export Review Board* to certify which artwork or other item has Canadian cultural significance. If the donation is certified *and* made to a designated institution there is no tax due on the disposition. Thus, if the charity is hoping to attract donations of property with a particular significance, it is important to secure the designation.

There are two categories of designation -

Category A is granted for an indefinite period of time to institutions that are well-established and meet all the criteria related to certain legal, curatorial and environmental requirements.

Category B is granted in relation to an institution involved in the proposed acquisition of an object (or collection) that does not meet all the criteria for designation, but which has demonstrated its capability to effectively preserve the type of property in question. More information on designation is available from the Department of Canadian Heritage.

The criteria by which the Board makes its decisions is beyond the scope of this book, but the Board can be contacted to provide a review at:

Canadian Cultural Property Export Review Board
Department of Canadian Heritage
15 Eddy Street, 3rd Floor
Gatineau, QC
Phone: (819) 997-7761
www.pch.gc.ca/progs/cebc-cperb/index-e.cfm

As a proper certification may involve many months' worth of research, a request for certification should be made well before the donation is contemplated.

If a taxpayer donates certified property to a designated institution, there will not be any tax owing on the gift. In addition, the taxpayer is entitled to a tax receipt for 100% of the value of the gift (as determined by the Board).

Example:

Noa owns a first edition Captain Canada comic book that she purchased for $50,000. Noa, realizing that it might be of significant cultural value, asks the *Canadian Cultural Property Export Review Board* to assess the comic book. The Board does so and determines that the comic book is indeed of cultural value and that its fair market value is $100,000.

Noa then contacts the charity she has in mind, which happily agrees to accept the donation but confesses that they do not have "designated institution" status. In calculating her tax situation on donating the comic book, Noa does the following calculation:

Proceeds of Disposition:	$ 100,000
Cost Base	$ 50,000
Capital Gain	$ 50,000
Taxes Owing	$ 23,000
Tax Credit	$ 46,000
Net Taxes	0
Leftover Credit	$ 23,000

Realizing that she would have to pay $23,000 of tax on the gift, Noa contacts another charity, which does qualify as a designated institution. On this donation she would have no net taxes and a leftover credit of $46,000. Clearly, Noa has an incentive to choose the designated charity. This incentive only increases in proportion to the value of the gift.

These significant tax benefits were designed to encourage Canadians to donate cultural properties to Canadian institutions, and thereby ensure that significant art and cultural objects remain in Canada. It should be noted that the program applies to items which are of cultural significance, not just Canadian culture. The rules also apply where such a gift is made by Will.

PROPERTY DONATED BY ARTIST

An artist who produces artwork for sale is considered to be producing inventory for a business. In this regard, the donation of artwork is considered a donation of inventory and treated as such (see below). Nevertheless, any artwork produced by an artist may qualify as Canadian cultural property regardless of whether it was produced for resale. When there is a gift or bequest of such cultural property, the rules described above with regard to such gifts will apply even though the property is not a capital asset.

INVENTORY

The determination of whether an item is inventory or capital is one of the most fundamental areas of our income tax system, but nevertheless is shrouded in vagueness and controversy. For example, to most people a house is a capital property, but if the owner of the home is engaged in the business of buying and selling homes the property becomes inventory of a business, and the question becomes, "When is one engaged in a business?" As discussed in Chapter 1, the distinction is important because only 50% of the gain of capital property is taxable as opposed to 100% of the profit on inventory being taxable. Thus, in this context, there is a strong incentive for individuals to classify an item as capital instead of inventory. That said, the donation of inventory will result in tax credits that will at least offset the tax due on the disposition of the inventory.

Example:

Mia runs a business making stuffed animals. Her business is not incorporated, so all the income of the business is taxed at her personal rates during the year.

After Mia has deducted all of her expenses, she is left with taxable income in the year of $50,000. If Mia sells one more toy that is worth $100, she will pay tax on that toy of $31 (at her tax bracket). However, on donating the toy, she will be entitled to tax credits of approximately $40 (assuming that she has already made at least $200 of donations). Mia can then offset the tax owed by donating the last toy and using the additional $9 against the tax owing on her other $50,000 of income.

Of course, as income grows so too does the tax owing. In all provinces except Alberta, at the highest combined bracket the credits from the donation would just offset the tax owing and there would be no additional tax credits leftover for use. In Alberta however, the credits will always more than offset the tax on the disposition of the donated item, even at the highest brackets. Given the number of provinces, the multiplicity of tax rates and brackets and the frequency with which they change, it is impossible to include a comprehensive chart showing the tax treatment of all donations of inventory in this book. An accountant should be retained to calculate the results of any donation of inventory.

PERSONAL USE PROPERTY

As we have seen, the ITA only allows for the receipting of property and creates several classifications for property. Each class is accorded a different tax treatment. One such class is *Personal Use Property* (PUP), property that is owned by the taxpayer and that is primarily for the personal use and enjoyment of the taxpayer or persons related to the taxpayer. PUP includes:

- Bottles of wine
- Aeroplan points
- Air Miles
- Shoppers Optimum points
- Religious items
- Gift certificates
- Clothes
- Artwork
- Hobby items
- Comic books
- Model trains
- Toys
- Land (e.g. a fishing hole)
- Books

Normally, when these types of items are donated to a charity, the charity does not issue a receipt nor does the owner expect one. This is, in most cases, the appropriate treatment. However, technically it does not have to be so.

The ITA specifies that for donations of PUP, the minimum cost is deemed to be $1,000. This is true regardless of the actual cost to the owner. The ITA also deems the item sold for a minimum of $1,000, again regardless of the actual sale/donation value.[6] So, when taken into the donor's tax return, there is no taxable event on items that are worth less than $1000.

On the other hand, a tax receipt can still be issued for these types of items. The value on the receipt would reflect the item's *fair market value*. This receipt could then be used to generate some tax credits on the return (small though they may be). Charities should note though that valuing household items can be very difficult and receipts should only be issued if value can be defensibly determined.

Example 1

Jonah bought a "Tickle Me Elmo" doll for $20. Shortly thereafter, it became a collector's item and the fair market value increased to $100. Realizing that there are needy children without a Tickle Me Elmo, Jonah donates the toy to a local charity. In return, he receives a tax receipt for the value of $100. On his tax return he calculates his capital gain as follows:

Deemed Proceeds of Disposition	$ 1,000
Deemed Cost	- $ 1,000
Capital Gain	0

As there is no capital gain there is no tax payable. On the other hand, Jonah will receive a tax receipt for the fair market value of the doll ($100). Applying our assumptions (i.e. a tax rate of 46% and Jonah has already made at least $200 of donations), the $100 receipt will allow Jonah to claim back $46 of taxes owing from other sources.

The implication of this policy is that when items are donated which have an actual value greater than $1,000 but a cost lower than $1,000, the value of the donation will be enhanced because the amount of the capital gain will be reduced.

Example 2

Elliot decides to donate a model train set which he purchased for $100, but has it appraised in advance and discovers to his delight that it is actually worth

6 See Chapter 4 for more information regarding valuations.

$2,000. Elliot still decides to donate the train set to a willing charity, which issues him a receipt for $2,000. He then calculates his taxes as follows:

Actual Proceeds of Disposition	$	2,000
Deemed Cost	$	1,000
Capital Gain	$	1,000
Tax	$	230
Tax Credits	$	920
Total leftover credits	$	690

There are three notes to make about the type of property donated.

First, make sure that the property is actually transferable. While premium points are property, some plans will not allow you to transfer the points to anyone else, and so they effectively cannot be donated. In this scenario, a donor may consider redeeming the points and then donating the actual item. Of course, this may prove to be of limited assistance to a charity that all of a sudden finds itself obligated to use a plane ticket to some place it did not want to go, on a date it did not want to travel.

Second, both the individual and the charity must be careful about obtaining a reliable valuation. From the perspective of the individual, an improper valuation could lead to a donation tax credit disallowed by the CRA. The charity, on the other hand, has an obligation to issue proper receipts, so if the receipts are over-valued the charity may find itself facing uncomfortable questions from the CRA.

Finally, there are rules in the ITA which prevent situations where donors are buying and donating items that fall below the $1000 threshold simply to create tax receipts to shelter income from other sources. While the charity will not necessarily be punished if involved in such a scenario, the donor could have the receipt disallowed.

LISTED PERSONAL PROPERTY

Listed personal property (LPP) is a subclass of PUP. It consists of certain specific items which are held both as an investment and as hobby items. The list includes artwork, stamps, books, coins and sculptures. Unless it is *Certified Canadian Cultural Property* (see earlier in this chapter) LPP has the same tax treatment as PUP.

REAL ESTATE

Generally, the donation of most real estate will be treated like the donation of any other type of capital property. If the item is inventory the donor will be taxed on the full proceeds of disposition, and if the item is capital the donor will only pay tax on fifty percent of the proceeds of disposition. That said, there are two significant exceptions to this rule.

a. Principal residence

The first exception is the donation of the principal residence. Canadian residents are not taxed on the gain arising from the appreciation of their principal residence. So, if a donor bought his home for $100,000 and sells (or donates) the property when it is worth $1,000,000 no tax will be payable on the appreciation in value (assuming the home was the donor's principal residence for that entire time).

If the donor were to donate the home to a charity, not only would the donor have no tax consequences on the disposition but the donor would also receive a tax receipt equal to the fair market value of the home at the time of the donation. This can be useful for individuals who wish to offset any income they may have in the year of the donation or in the five following years (or in the two preceding years in the case of a bequest). However, depending on the amount of income the individual has, they might not be able to use the full amount of the receipt. This is especially true given that most Canadians have the bulk of their accumulated wealth tied up in the value of their homes. In some cases, it might make sense for the donor to leave their home to a charity in their Will. By doing this, the donor might be able to use the tax credits from the donation to offset the income from the deemed disposition of their other assets and carry back the credits to the previous year. In both the year of death and the year preceding death, the estate can use the tax credits to offset up to one hundred percent of the income. Given that the deemed disposition of assets (with the exception of the principal residence) usually results in a large income in the year of death the donor might, in fact, be able to do some significant tax planning in this way.

b. Environmental property

The donation of environmental property has a treatment similar to that of *Certified Cultural Property*. The treatment applies where property is designated as ecologically sensitive land by the Minister of the Environment (or a person designated by the Minister) and donated to any of:

- The Federal or Provincial Government
- A municipality in Canada
- A municipal or public body performing a function of government in Canada

- A registered charity that has a main purpose (in the opinion of that Minister) of conserving and protecting Canada's environmental heritage and that is approved by that minister or that person in respect of the gift.

In any of these cases, there will be no taxable capital gain on the donation.

As we have described the specific tax treatment of items donated where there is no tax on the capital gain of the item in the sections on public securities and certified cultural property there is no need to do it here. The only significant difference is that tax credits generated from a donation of this type may be carried forward for ten years. Suffice it to say that the entire value of the donation is available to offset tax owing from other sources at the highest rates.

Environmental charities may want to suggest to potential donors that the tax benefits of reclaiming the property for the environment (prior to donation) may outweigh the costs of bringing it to the Minister of the Environment's standards. In this way, donors will pay for the costs of converting the property into ecological property (if possible) and will benefit from the absence of tax on the donation.

RESIDUAL INTERESTS

Most people who are familiar with the donation of property to charity do not realize that the bundle of rights that comes with the ownership of property can be divided in different ways. One of the ways to do this is to divide ownership of the property during one's life (called a life interest) from ownership on the death of that person (called a residual interest).

This is different from a property owner who owns the property and on death uses a Will to dispose of the property in a manner he or she sees fit because the owner in that circumstance can change their mind as they still own the property. Once the residual interest is sold or given away, the property will belong to the owner of the residual interest when the owner of the *life interest* dies and only the owner of the *residual interest* can change that. A donor might consider this course of action in situations where the owner wants to enjoy the income or use of the property during their lifetime and yet donate the property to the charity during their lifetime as opposed to on their death.

The value of the residual interest is calculated using an estimated value of the underlying property at the expected death of the donor (in itself determined from actuarial mortality tables) using present value dollars. This amount will be the value listed on the charity's receipt. Determining the fair market value of a property at the expected death of the owner at some point in the future is a complicated mathematical task best left to a qualified actuary and appraiser.

From a tax perspective, when the owner divides the rights and donates the residual interest, the donor would generally incur a tax consequence. The tax owing will be a function of the cost of purchasing those rights and their estimated value at the time of their disposition. Generally speaking this income will be treated as a capital gain.

Example:

Yechiel buys a cottage at the age of 50 for $100,000. He decides he would like a charity to have the property on his death but he would like to enjoy the cottage during his lifetime. More to the point, he would like to use the tax credits now and enjoy the satisfaction of having made the donation while living. Yechiel consults an appraiser and an actuary, who together predict that in Yechiel's expected year of death the property will be worth $250,000 in today's dollars. Yechiel then donates the residual interest in the property to the charity. This entitles the charity to ownership of the property on Yechiel's death. In return, Yechiel receives a tax receipt for $250,000 which he can use against his taxes owing in this year and in the five following years. Even better, Yechiel is entitled to the income stream from the property should he decide to rent out the cottage during his lifetime.

Generally, there will be tax on the disposition of the residual interest (unless the property is, for example, a principal residence or ecological property being donated to an ecological charity). The capital gain is calculated according to a specific formula and depends on the gain in value of the residual interest relative to the entire property.

So, if Yechiel owned the property for some time before donating the residual interest, the tax calculation can become quite complex as it involves not only an estimate of the value of the property at the expected date of disposition but also a relative assignment of the cost of the property to the residual interest according to a specific formula. In any case involving the donation of residual interests it is best to consult an experienced professional.

It should be noted that while technically the charity may pay for the maintenance and upkeep of the property, this is typically absorbed by the donor. Nevertheless, this should be the subject of a comprehensive agreement between the donor and the charity. Furthermore, the charity may want to make a notation on the title deed of the property indicating that it owns the residual interest, but even if the property is real estate not every jurisdiction allows this.

CHARITABLE REMAINDER TRUST

A trust is a legal device which effectively accomplishes one or both of the following objectives:

1. It separates the ownership of property (the capital interest) from the right to receive income from the property (the income interest), and
2. It can separate the person who legally controls the property from those entitled to benefit from it.

A Charitable Remainder Trust (CRT) is similar to the donation of a residual interest in that it allows the donor to donate the capital of the trust now, but the charity does not receive it until some later point (such as on the death of the donor). A CRT is particularly useful in situations where it is difficult to record the division of interests on title (such as artwork). Despite its legal potency, creating a CRT is simply a matter of signing the appropriate legal documents.

When a donor creates a CRT, he or she disposes of property to the trust and then donates an interest in the trust to the charity. It is important to note that the donation in this case occurs when the owner transfers the interest in the trust to the charity. Thus, if the underlying property is, for example, publicly traded securities, the gift of an interest in the trust will not attract the same favourable tax treatment as donating the securities would have; it is a donation of an interest in a trust, not of securities.

The special tax treatment assigned to different types of property outlined elsewhere in this chapter, such as ecological property, publicly traded securities or certified cultural property, likely makes them inappropriate candidates for this type of donation.

It is important not to create the trust with the charity as the beneficiary, because if the donor is not careful he or she will gift an interest in the trust with no property (and thus no value on the receipt). Any subsequent disposition to the trust will not be considered a gift by the CRA. The appropriate method is instead to create the trust with the donor holding both interests in the trust. The donor then contributes the assets to the trust, and finally donates the capital interest to the charity. Of course, the donor would retain the income interest for herself as long as is set out in the trust deed.

As the tax consequences are similar to those experienced with a gift of residual interest, they are not explored here.

INVENTORIES OF MEDICINE

In the 2007 budget, the government enacted a provision whereby Canadian companies which donate inventory of medications to certain charities were entitled to an additional deduction as a way to encourage the donation of these medications. Unfortunately, the deduction only applied if the donation was made to a charity which had received a disbursement under a program of the *Canadian International Development Agency* (CIDA) and the donation was made for use outside of Canada. This definition is fraught with difficulties in terms of both available information and timing.

Ostensibly to simplify matters, the 2008 budget changed the qualifications for a charity to one where, in the opinion of the Minister responsible for CIDA, the charity meets a list of requirements prescribed from time to time by regulations attached to the ITA. The thrust of these regulations will be to ensure that eligible charities:

- act in a manner consistent with the principles and objectives of the World Health Organization Guidelines for Drug Donations;
- have expertise in delivering medical donations to the developing world; and
- implement appropriate policies and practices with respect to the delivery of international development assistance.

GIFTS FROM U.S. DONORS

Individuals who reside in Canada and commute to their employment or place of business in the United States are allowed to deduct donations made to U.S. charitable organizations on the same terms as those made to Canadian organizations.

There are, however, a number of other important conditions which must be met. First, the commuter must live near the American border during the whole of the taxation year. Secondly, his U.S. employment or business income must represent his chief source of income for that year. Thirdly, he must be able to demonstrate that the gift was made to a religious, charitable, scientific, literary or educational organization created or organized in or under the laws of the United States. Finally, he or she must be able to demonstrate that such a gift would be allowed as a deduction under the United States Internal Revenue Code. Where all those conditions are met, the donations in question are treated as donations made to a registered charity.

VOLUNTEER SERVICES

The ITA makes it very clear that only a gift to a charity is receiptable. As explained elsewhere, a gift includes property or a right to property. Unfortunately, services do not qualify as property and, therefore are not receiptable.

This affects many different aspects of running a charity. For example, a painter who volunteers his services to paint the wall of a church cannot receive a receipt for the time he spent doing the painting. He can be reimbursed for the costs of his supplies but, of course, this is a separate matter. If, for some reason, the volunteer requires a receipt, the appropriate thing to do is to have an exchange of cheques for the services and the donation. So, in our example, the painter would invoice the charity for the amount of his or her work and the charity would pay the individual for the work. The painter would then turn around and write a separate cheque to the charity in the amount of the donation to the charity. In this way, the painter will have to claim as income the amount of the invoice and will get an offsetting deduction for the donation. In all provinces except Alberta there will be a small net benefit to the painter if the painter is not in the highest tax bracket, with this effect getting bigger as the donor's income gets smaller. In Alberta, however, because the top tax credit rate on donations is actually higher than the top marginal income tax rate, such a plan would actually result in the volunteer coming out somewhat ahead regardless of his income.

LOAN BACKS

In the context of donations there are really only two types of loan arrangements which involve charities. The first involves the donation of a gift and then the loan back of funds to the donor or someone who is non arm's-length to the donor. In these cases, the value of the receipt may be reduced by the amount of the benefit returned to the donor.

The other area in which loans involving charities occur, involve the loan of capital items, generally artwork, from a donor to a charity. In these cases, donors often have a particular item of interest and want to enjoy it for their lifetime. For example, the owner may be prepared to donate the item to charity but wish to display the item in their home for as long as they live. Assuming the donor does not use a CRT to do this, the owner would donate the item to a charity and receive a receipt based on the fair market value of the donation. The receipt would be reduced by the value of the loan back to the shareholder. It is important for charities to know that these types of arrangements are possible but note that the valuation calculation is a complicated task best left to experienced professionals.

6

Revenue and Receipting

Many people confuse the term charity with the term not-for-profit. Technically, these are different types of organizations. A not-for-profit, as the name would imply, cannot organize its affairs in order to earn a profit. A charity on the other hand *can* earn profit and generally engage in business relationships outside of simply obtaining donations. Examples of such activities include gift shops in hospitals and churches, charity bake sales and even rental income of property owned by charities. However, because charities are not taxable, Parliament has legislated limits to their involvement in the business world to ensure that charities do not take advantage of this status to create an unlevel playing field with taxable businesses.

Charities also raise funds in other ways and due to their charitable status these methods often involve the issuance of a charitable donation tax receipt. But, in order to maintain the integrity of the charitable donation tax credit mechanism, the law contains a series of complicated provisions which apply in various situations. This is clearly necessary as every donation tax receipt issued involves foregone tax revenue on the part of the government and so it is important to ensure that receipts are only issued for gifts to charity. This chapter will review the rules regarding the different types of revenue a charity may receive, and outline some of the most common concerns regarding the issue of proper receipts.

BUSINESS REVENUE

As stated in the introduction, there are concerns about allowing a non-taxable entity to compete without restrictions against for-profit corporations. This is not a trifling matter as for-profit organizations are the backbone of our economy.

On the other hand, it would be unfairly capricious to deny a charity the ability to earn revenue off of its assets - particularly as the income is generally used to support charitable activities. And more to the point, there is significant revenue to be gained from involvement in the business world that can be put to good use in a charity - albeit with the accompanying concern regarding the risk to which charitable assets are exposed in the business world.

Charities are restricted from carrying out business that is unrelated to its charitable purposes where that business is substantially run by people employed by the charity. As a result, the first exception to running a business is one that is primarily run by volunteers or by people that are effectively contracted to run the enterprise. Unfortunately most people that are involved in running a business are, by definition, paid employees. And the exception for businesses run by volunteers is effectively limited to small operations of organizations with large volunteer bases.

On the other hand, a charity *may* run a business that is related to the charity's purposes and subordinate to that purpose. The first question that must be answered is whether or not the activity is in fact a business. For many organizations this determination will become necessary in separating a fundraising activity (a monthly bake sale) from a business activity (running a gift shop). Most of the guidance on the application of these rules is administrative (as opposed to statutory or common law), a copy of the CRA guidance on this topic is available at **www.runningacharity.ca**.

Not all commercial activity is necessarily a business. For example, there is a distinction between a bake sale and running a bakery. A business is a commercial activity deriving revenue from the sale of goods or services undertaken with the intention to profit from this activity. There are certain indicators which may be found in running a business. They are:

a. Intention: the purpose of the activity intended to generate a profit.
b. The potential to show profit: just because a business is unsuccessful does not mean that the operators did not have the intention and the ability to make a profit at some point. On the other hand, if the endeavour is structured so that it could never earn a profit then presumably it is not a business.
c. History of profit: just because an activity has fallen onto hard times, does not mean that the history of earning profit would be ignored.
d. The expertise of the people undertaking the activity: if the people who run the activity have experience and a history of running such for-profit activities, that would be an indicator that this may also be intended to be a commercial endeavor.

It should be noted that neither soliciting donations nor selling donated goods is necessarily considered to be a commercial activity; although one could imagine circumstances where these types of activities could be part of a larger business. It should also be noted that just because fees are charged for the provision of certain charitable programs does not necessarily mean that the program will constitute a business. For example, accepting rent for low-income housing, or university tuition would not qualify the supplier charity as a business. However, the CRA does have certain economic development policies which should be consulted if the organization intends to engage in such activities as micro finance or employment of the hard to employ.

Another issue to keep in mind is the frequency with which the activity is carried on. For example, a charity may decide to engage in an auction of purchased equipment. Conducting such an event once is unlikely to attract the CRA's attention. However, conducting this activity on a regular basis would – assuming the other criteria are also present – be a cause for some concern. But the law in this area is not entirely clear and there is no bright line test to suggest how much activity is too much. From a policy perspective, conducting an activity once would likely not create the same level of concern with respect to competition with for-profit entities as conducting the activity on a regular basis. As the line between fundraising events and business becomes more distinct, the charity will run a greater risk of attracting unwanted CRA attention.

A. Related to charitable purposes

The issue of a link between the organization's charitable purposes and the business being proposed should not be overlooked. That the income generated from a business activity is then applied to an organization's charitable purposes is insufficient to form a link. The activity itself must be linked to the charitable purposes of the organization. The CRA has identified four forms of connection. If the business falls into one of these categories it will be considered to be a business that is linked to the charitable purpose.

The first type is that the activity is a usual and necessary component of charitable programs. Put another way, these activities are generally necessary in order to conduct the charity's operations. For example, a hospital that has a parking lot, cafeteria or gift shop for use of patrons of the hospital. University bookstores and school uniform shops are also all considered necessary programs to improve the quality of the service delivered by the charity.

The second type of connection is activities that are an off-shoot of a charitable program. In these cases the operation of the charity creates marketable goods as an off-shoot but not necessarily as the core programming of the organization. For example, an organization that intends to teach developmentally disabled adults life skills may produce artwork for sale; or an agricultural exhibit may produce flour or fruits and vegetables which could be available for purchase.

Third, the charity may have excess capacity as a result of the general operation of its core programming. Clearly charities require physical space and staff in order to operate. At times they may have excess capacity which it cannot use for any purpose. In these circumstances the charity would be well within its rights to rent out some of this capacity. For example, a charity may, in order to meet municipal regulations, be required to add residential accommodations to its premises. Unless the charity provides low-income housing, this is excess capacity which can be rented out to members of the public (one would have to be careful of the undue benefit rules). Another example may include a church that once had a Sunday school program which is now discontinued. That space could now be rented to some other school in full compliance with the law.

Fourth, the sale of items that promote the charity is clearly linked with the organization's charitable purposes. For example, Mothers Against Drunk Driving may create bumper stickers intended to remind people not to drink and drive. The sale of these bumper stickers would be linked to MADD's objects.

B. Subordinate

In addition to being related to the organizations' charitable purposes, the business must be subordinate to the charity's real mission of undertaking good works. In other words just because the activities are linked, does not mean they can overtake a charity's general operations. Unfortunately this test is somewhat subjective. Nevertheless, if one is faced with a CRA audit it will be important to be able to show that the resources used in the business (including volunteer time) are a relatively small part of the charity's overall work. The CRA has four indicators it uses to determine whether or not an activity is subordinate to the charity's main purpose.

First, a subjective analysis of whether or not the business activity is a minor portion of the charity's attention and resources. The difficulty in applying this test is apparent with respect to a volunteer's time. How is that to be determined as a measure of the resources available to the charity? That said, the CRA may look at the amount of time spent at board meetings discussing these issues or the allocation of an employee's time in managing a business. In certain circumstances if the endeavour is taking up an unusual amount of time this may be related to a temporary circumstance (such as a bumper crop, or unexpected business opportunity) which should be brought to the CRA's attention.

Second, the CRA will look to see whether or not the business is integrated into the charity's operations or if it is acting as a self-contained unit. (This question may be related to that involving excess capacity). Obviously, if the business is a self-contained operation it is likely unrelated to the organization's charitable purpose but even if it is related, it may not be subordinate to the organization's activities.

Third, an analysis as to whether the organization's charitable goals continue to dominate its decision-making. Over time all organizations are subject to mission creep, that is the phenomenon where new activities tend to dominate the agenda of the group. It is important where the organization does engage in some business activity that it remember that it is a charitable organization dedicated to pursuing its charitable purposes.

Finally, the organization must be certain to continue to pursue its charitable purposes and allow no element of private benefit to enter into its operations. While technically not an issue of subordination, it may be cause for revocation of the charitable registration if, for example, the organization provides salaries which are overly high or employs more people than is necessary to conduct its business.

Sometimes, the CRA latches onto business-related issues because they are anomalous in the charity's overall operation. That they are anomalous should itself be a clue that the organization is perhaps overextending itself. Generally, this can happen where the charity is forced into a situation it did not foresee. One example may be a situation where, in order to comply with municipal law, a charity is required to provide additional parking spaces in front of its building on a busy commercial street. Unfortunately, providing such spaces was impossible so it acquired an additional building on the block to allow it to meet the municipal requirement. Then, left with a building for which it had no need, the charity proceeded to rent the building out; thus engaging in an activity which was not related to its objects (the subordinate issue is another matter altogether).

The point to take from this true story is that a charity can easily be caught up in related business issues by following the law (in this case municipal). It is therefore critical for charities to be aware of the various pitfalls that await when engaging in different types of revenue generating activities.

INVESTMENT INCOME

Many charities have endowments. An endowment effectively is a sum of money which is invested as capital in order to create income to support the charities operations. Clearly the investment of such income is an allowable activity on the part of charities. However, charities need to be extremely careful in investing their funds as the protection of charitable property is of prime concern for the law generally.

As a preliminary point, it should be noted that directors of charities have a duty to act prudently with respect to the charity's assets. This does not mean that the charity cannot lose money in an investment. Prudent investments can sometimes lose money and risky investments can make money. Nevertheless, decisions must be made so that charitable assets are invested after due consideration and diligent review. Most provinces have rules in place (within their respective Trustee Acts) regarding certain behaviors involved in investments. For example, Ontario has rules involving the delegation of decisions to investment counsel. Any organization with a sufficiently large endowment should speak to qualified legal counsel to determine what their legal responsibilities may be. This is particularly true as directors can remain personally responsible for imprudent investments.

Investments can take a variety of forms. They can be government bonds, corporate bonds, common shares, preferred shares, loans and mortgages. Generally speaking, most of these investments are treated in the same way. Once made the capital of these investments become subject to the disbursement quota rules described elsewhere in this book. This rule effectively requires these investments to earn approximately 3.5% in return to satisfy the disbursement quota in the following year without eating into the capital of the endowment.

Investment in shares of an operating business may run into certain other restrictions. In particular, a private foundation would be limited from holding certain shares under the excess business holding rules. These rules would effectively require a less than 2% holding in such a business but the excess business holding rules do not apply to public foundations or registered charities.

All charities need to be careful about accepting donations of *non-qualifying securities*. These are generally shares or bonds of private corporations. By their very nature they tend to be illiquid and hard to sell. As a result, the *Income Tax Act* contains certain rules regarding receipting by certain charities and effectively do not allow a charity the ability to receipt such items unless they are sold within five years of their receipt. Rules surrounding non-qualifying securities are complicated and qualified counsel should be sought if the charity is approached for a donation of this type. The rules are explained in greater detail elsewhere in this book.

SPONSORSHIPS

Many charities attract sponsorships from corporate donors. To the extent that the donors receive value for service, the contribution is not receiptable. This raises the difficulty of attaching a value to the service the donor receives. For example, how much is an ad in a charity's bulletin worth? Just because the charity charges $100 does not necessarily mean that it is really $100 worth of value.

A donor that is a corporation is in the same after-tax position regardless of whether it donates funds to a charity or it makes a business deduction. That is to say, a donation tax receipt is a deduction of the same amount as an equal business expense. For this reason the CRA and most businesses are often flexible about valuation. If the donor paid $10,000 for an advertisement which could only be valued at $5,000, then technically a charitable donation tax receipt should be issued for the other $5,000. However, (to take the two possible extremes) if a business was issued a receipt for the full $10,000 it would have the same net tax effect as if no tax receipt were issued and the corporation made a deduction for a business expense of the full amount. Nevertheless, the law does allow a charity to issue a receipt for the amount donated less the value of the good return. In valuing these advertisements (for example) the charity should consult with an accountant who may be able to provide specific advice in those circumstances.

PURCHASING FOR THE PURPOSE OF DONATING

Generally speaking, receipts reflect the full fair market value of the item being donated. (A discussion of the meaning of fair market value can be found later in this chapter.) However, certain rules exist for situations where the donor has purchased something for the express purpose of donating it to the charity under the terms of a gifting arrangement. A gifting arrangement is effectively a tax shelter arrangement where a donor is encouraged to buy at a low price and donate for a high valuation. In these circumstances, where the purchase was made less than three years before the day that the gift was made, or where the property was purchased less than ten years ago, (but it is reasonable to conclude that when it was acquired one of the main reasons for that acquisition was to donate to the charity) the charity must issue a receipt for the *lesser* of the fair market value of the property or the cost of the property to the donor.

While the charity does not have to undertake superhuman efforts to determine the date which the property was acquired, or the value at which it was acquired, it would be sensible for the charity to at least make basic inquiries of the donor. There are certain exceptions to this rule, they include:

- Inventory
- Canadian real-estate
- Shares of publicly traded corporations
- Ecological property
- Canadian cultural property export review board certified property
- Certain other shares or property of a corporation which is acquired in exchange for property which would otherwise be exempt from the receipting rule.

SPLIT RECEIPTING

As already stated, a charity must issue a receipt for the full fair market value of items donated to it. However, in circumstances where the donor receives some benefit in return for his or her donation, the charity must reduce the amount on the receipt by the value returned to the donor. It bears mentioning that the rules also include a benefit returned to anybody not at arm's length to the donor. For example, if a charity is hosting a banquet and sells seats for $250 but provides a meal for $50 and entertainment worth $25 the value of the receipt of $250 must be reduced by $75 being the value of the benefits returned to the donor.

The difficulty which arises in this circumstance is valuing the benefit returned to the donor. This is particularly true as the amounts contemplated are often very small. Where the issue involves large benefits returned (such as might be the case in corporate sponsorships) a certified valuator can be retained. For small amounts, such as the value of entertainment at a charity banquet, issuing a valuation can be rather difficult. In these circumstances it is worthwhile to speak with an accountant about the proper criteria for making such a valuation. The same would be true of any circumstance in which the charity returns a benefit to the donor either directly or indirectly. The goal here is not only to properly issue a receipt but also to show the CRA that the charity was diligent in obtaining a reasonable – and defensible – valuation.

WHAT GOES ON THE RECEIPT

We often encounter specific questions about what goes on the receipt. The rules in this regard are clear; the receipt must clearly show, in a manner that cannot readily be altered:

(*a*) the name and address in Canada of the organization as recorded with the CRA;

(*b*) the registration number assigned by the CRA to the charity;

(*c*) the serial number of the receipt;

(*d*) the place or locality where the receipt was issued;

(*e*) where the gift is a cash gift, the date on which or the year during which the gift was received;

(*e.1*) where the gift is of property other than cash;

(i) the date on which the gift was received

(ii) a brief description of the property
(iii) the name and address of the appraiser of the property if an appraisal is done

(*f*) the date on which the receipt was issued;

(*g*) the name and address of the donor including, in the case of an individual, the individual's first name and initial;

(*h*) the amount that is
(i) the amount of a cash gift, or
(ii) if the gift is of property other than cash, the amount that is the fair market value of the property at the time that the gift is made;

(*h.1*) a description of the benefit returned to the donor, if any, in respect of the gift and the amount of that benefit;

(*h.2*) the eligible amount of the gift;

(*i*) the signature, of a responsible individual who has been authorized by the organization to acknowledge gifts (facsimile signatures are allowed);

(*j*) the name and Internet website of the Canada Revenue Agency (**www.cra.gc.ca**).

It bears mentioning that a receipt can include more than this and should the charity wish to use the issuance of a receipt for any additional purpose, (such as thanking the donor or soliciting future donations), statements of this type may be included.

WHO GETS THE RECEIPT

Charities are sometimes given a cheque from a donor corporation but asked to issue a receipt to an individual. *The charity should not participate in such arrangements*. Receipts should be issued in the name of the donor. This means that if the donor is a corporation the receipt should be issued to that corporation as evidenced by the name on the cheque. In cases where it is impossible to tell who the actual donor is, the charity should be able to rely on the word of the person making the actual physical transfer. This would be the case in situations involving cash.

WHEN IS THE RECEIPT ISSUED?

The receipt can be issued as soon as the gift is made. This is true even where there may be a condition subsequent to the gift. However if the charity wishes to delay the issuance of receipts it can do so. This may happen where the charity is expecting regular monthly donations and wants to issue one global receipt for all of them. By way of CRA guidelines, charities can issue receipts as late as the end of February. While there is no formal law on the point, most donors appreciate receiving receipts sooner rather than later.

REPLACING A RECEIPT

From time to time a charity will issue a receipt which is then misplaced or accidentally destroyed by the donor. In these cases, the charity can reissue a receipt so long as it contains all of the required information, the serial number of the original receipt (and the new receipt) and a statement that it replaces the original receipt.

The copy of the original receipt kept by the charity should be marked with a note that it has been cancelled. The same process can be followed if a charity issued a receipt with incorrect information.

RETURNING GIFTS

Sometimes charities face the prospect of returning a gift to a donor. There are two ways this may arise. The first is where the donor, or the donor's family, request that the gift be returned. In these circumstances, a charity should know that returning a gift to a donor may put the charity off-side the rules regarding transfers to non-qualified donees. In other words, the charity may not be able to return the gift to the donor even if it wants to do so.

In other circumstances, the charity may wish to return the gift to the donor because the donor has committed some sort of public act with which the charity does not want to be associated. This happened famously in the case of David Radler, a former associate of Conrad Black's who made a large donation to Queens University and in return Queens put Mr. Radler's name on a wing of its business school. The day after Mr. Radler pleaded guilty to fraud charges in the U.S. Queens decided that they could no longer in good conscience be associated with Mr. Radler and attempted to return the gift to him.

Provisions within the *Income Tax Act* allow for the CRA to go back and reassess an individual who obtained the benefit of a charitable receipt for a gift which is then later returned. However, the obligation to not bestow a benefit on a non-qualified donee continues to exist. Thus, the situations in which a charity may be able to return a gift to a donor are typically those where there is a lasting condition attached to the gift which eventually allows the charity to return the gift if the condition is not met.

These conditions are usually rare as charities do not usually contemplate the return of a gift to the donor. However, if the charity is going to remain associated with the donor or the donor's family for a lasting period of time then it may be wise to contemplate such a clause at the time of the gift in order that an option exists into the future.

7

CRA Regulations

Given that the regulation of charities lies predominantly in the *Federal Income Tax Act*, it may surprise many in the nonprofit community to know that regulation of the sector is inherently a provincial responsibility and not a federal one. That this is so, is primarily a matter of history (and the almost complete abdication by the Provinces of their responsibilities). However, as regulation of the sector does fall to the CRA, the dispute resolution process tends to follow the same general framework as that for private taxpayers. This also extends to the filing of an annual information return similar to a tax return; the use of terms defined in the *Income Tax Act* are generally for other purposes but are also applicable to the regulation of charities and the calculation of monetary penalties.

It should also be understood that the CRA's main mandate is to protect the integrity of the income tax base. Charities, by virtue of the donation tax credit, detract from that base so there is an inherent conflict within the CRA between these two duties. This is not to say that the CRA has any incentive to revoke the registration of charities in order that its other mandate may be met, but rather that the people who enforce the law through the CRA are generally trained for the primary mandate rather than this secondary one.

This chapter attempts to describe some of the various issues which may arise in interacting with the CRA as a charity attempts to meet its responsibilities under the *Income Tax Act*.

T3010

The annual information return to be filed by charities within six months of their year-end is called the registered charity information return. It is form T3010 available on the CRA website or **www.runningacharity.ca** and is generally mailed through conventional means to every charity prior to the deadline for filing. In the mailing, the CRA includes identification stickers for the submitted draft of the T3010. While the CRA prefers that the barcodes are used, this is not absolutely necessary should the charity misplace them.

The T3010 document is designed for a CRA official to review and spot any obvious inconsistencies with the law. Of course, given the number of charities and the volume of information reported on the T3010, the Charities Directorate simply does not have the person power available to review these documents in anything but the most cursory way and so only does so in any meaningful way prior to an audit.

Once received by the Charities Directorate, an officer will review the document to be sure that it is completed correctly and fully. The information in the document will then be posted online - with the exception of certain confidential information such as the addresses of the directors. Making the information in the T3010 available to the public can pose certain public relations problems for charities generally related to examination of their administrative expenses relative to the charitable expenses of the organization. Confusion about these expenses is compounded by the fact that the T3010 does not request standardized financial information but rather information that is of use for fulfilling the CRA's goal of determining whether or not the organization is in compliance with the law. For example, a typical income statement and balance sheet is not posted with the T3010.

Moreover, much of the information reported on the T3010 contains a subjective legal element - such as reporting of the organization's involvement in political activity - requiring the charity to make a legal determination regarding the characterization of the activity. And for the general reader, understanding non-standardized information with a legal judgment element – especially where the reader *does not know there is a subjective judgment* in the mix almost inevitably results in confusion.

There has been some significant criticism and even a number of public relations problems caused by information (some of it even accurately filed) little understood by the reader. It is therefore critical that when filing their T3010, charities try to file the information with an eye towards what a third-party would understand when reading the information. For this reason, it is often useful to engage the services of an accountant or other financial professional who has experience in standardized reporting.

The T3010 document itself asks a number of rather specific questions that move from an identification of the charity and the people that run it to a brief description of its programs and finally a detailed list of questions on its financial transactions. The CRA publishes a guide to completing the T3010 document, called the T0433 and it explains, in detail, each step required in completing both the document and its numerous schedules.

The structures of the T3010 and its subjective nature prevents us from providing a step-by-step description of completing the T3010. It should suffice to leave the charity with two warnings. First, keep in mind that the T3010 document is a public document and much of the charity's reputation for prudent spending could evaporate upon a close inspection by the public of the document. For this reason, the document must be taken extremely seriously and specific questions should be directed to a professional charity advisor. Second, charities are required to file a full and complete return within the timeframe allocated for doing so. A charity which files an inaccurate return is subject to revocation and a charity which files a document beyond the time limit for doing so, may be automatically revoked for failure to file. Therefore, charities should begin the process of completing the return as soon as possible after their year-end to give them plenty of time to complete it fully and submit it on time. Generally this will also involve accurate bookkeeping throughout the year to make the filing as quick and painless as possible.

Providing information

There are two circumstances in which the charity may be asked to provide its financial information to the CRA. The first and most obvious involves submission of the annual return. The second is an audit of the charity itself. When a charity is being audited, it must provide the information requested. Refusal to do so is an offence in and of itself, but in a charity context can also lead to the revocation of the charity's status under an accusation by the CRA that the charity has simply failed to maintain adequate books and records.

In an audit situation, the charity must provide all information requested by the CRA. Exceptions exist for items which may be subject to privilege. This is usually solicitor/client privilege of communications with a lawyer but certain other forms of privilege exist. If a charity is going to claim that certain documents are privileged and will not be released to the CRA, it should consult a lawyer both to ensure that the claim of privilege is valid and about the proper methods in ensuring privilege is maintained.

From time to time, the information contained in the charity's financial records may be of interest to the CRA in an investigation of other parties (generally donors). In these circumstances, the CRA may issue a *demand for information* regarding a particular donor(s) from a charity's files. The courts have generally held that the CRA has wide-ranging powers to request and receive information from a charity. This is not to say that a simple letter requesting information from the CRA must necessarily be complied with. There are legal steps by which the CRA can formally request documents of the organization. Depending on the nature of the request, it may indeed have the force of law and the charity may be compelled to reply. Again, legal counsel must be consulted to determine the charity's obligation to comply.

The release of information which may harm the financial interests of donors is, of course, a difficult decision for a charity. It is perhaps even more difficult when the release of such information may result in penalties against the directors of the charity themselves. For these reasons a charity which receives a request for information from the CRA may properly ask that the request be formally made. This would allow the charity to plausibly claim that it had no choice but to release the information.

DIRECTOR PENALTIES

In addition to the penalties described in Table 1, directors of charities, the charity itself, the individual signing receipts and any individual aware of a receipt issued with certain improprieties can become liable to a penalty under the *Income Tax Act*. The penalty is equal to 50% of the amount of the understated tax by the individual using the receipt. Generally, one would assume that to be the amount of the receipt multiplied by the highest marginal tax rate in the province (see Chapter 1) multiplied again by 50%. To our knowledge, these penalties have only been levied against individuals involved in tax shelters (in fact only one of these cases has ever gone to Court).

Directors are often concerned about the potential penalties that may be levelled against them and indeed these types of penalties (known as third-party penalties) are a concern. However, the law also requires some measure of the individual's intention to break the law for them to be liable for the penalty. Directors acting to their best ability to ensure compliance likely need not worry.

Directors can also become liable for a number of other legal obligations. This may include source deductions for tax, CPP and EI, employee wages, and environmental issues. It may also include obligations to ensure that charitable property is properly used, but these are all dealt with in a different manner and so do not form the subject matter of this book.

POTENTIAL PENALTIES

Effectively the *Income Tax Act* allows for charities to be revoked for even the smallest of transgressions. Realizing that this may be somewhat draconian, several years ago Parliament implemented a range of potential intermediate sanctions within the *Income Tax Act*. The sanctions from a variety of monetary penalties to suspension, annulment or revocation of a charity's status. A chart of these penalties is provided in Table 1. The CRA may also impose a compliance agreement on the charity which is described in fuller detail below.

Table 1 – List of Charity Penalties

Infraction	Penalty/Suspension for FIRST INFRACTION	Penalty/Suspension FOR REPEAT INFRACTIONS
Not filing an annual information return (Form T3010) on time	$500 penalty (assessed when an application for re-registration is made)	$500 penalty (assessed when an application for re-registration is made)
Issuing receipts with incomplete information	5% penalty on the eligible amount stated on the receipt	10% penalty on the eligible amount stated on the receipt
Not keeping proper books and records or not providing them to authorized CRA officials when requested	Suspension of tax-receipting privileges	Suspension of tax-receipting privileges
Charitable organization or public foundation carrying on an unrelated business	5% penalty on gross unrelated business revenue earned in a fiscal period	100% penalty on gross unrelated business revenue earned in a fiscal period and suspension of tax-receipting privileges
Private foundation carrying on a business	5% penalty on gross business revenue earned in a fiscal period	100% penalty on gross business revenue earned in a fiscal period and suspension of tax-receipting privileges
Foundation acquiring control of a corporation	5% penalty on dividends paid to the charity by the corporation	100% penalty on dividends paid to the charity by the corporation
Undue benefit provided by a charity to any person or entity (for example, a charity provides an interest-free loan to a director or non-qualified donee)	105% penalty on the amount of undue benefit	110% penalty on the amount of undue benefit. If the undue benefit is not conferred from a gift the suspension of tax-receipting privileges is also applicable.
Issuing receipts when there is no gift or when the receipt contains false information (when the total penalties **do not exceed** $25,000)	125% penalty on the eligible amount stated on the receipt	125% penalty on the eligible amount stated on the receipt

Table 1 – List of Charity Penalties

Infraction	Penalty/Suspension for FIRST INFRACTION	Penalty/Suspension FOR REPEAT INFRACTIONS
Issuing receipts when there is no gift or when the receipt contains false information (when the total penalties **exceed** $25,000)	125% penalty on the eligible amount stated on the receipt and suspension of tax-receipting privileges	125% penalty on the eligible amount stated on the receipt and suspension of tax-receipting privileges
Entering into a transaction, including making a gift to another registered charity, to delay expenditures on charitable activities	For the charities involved, a 110% penalty on the amount of the expenditure avoided or delayed	For the charities involved, a 110% penalty on the amount of the expenditure avoided or delayed
Accepting gifts or transfers of property on behalf of a suspended qualified donee	Suspension of tax-receipting privileges	Suspension of tax-receipting privileges
Private foundation not divesting itself of a percentage of its shares at the end of its fiscal period, in respect of a class of shares	5% of the result of multiplying the divestment obligation percentage of the private foundation for the fiscal period by the fair market value of all issued and outstanding shares in that class, except when there is a repeat infraction or another penalty for not disclosing, as indicated below, that applies for the fiscal period	10% of the result of multiplying the divestment obligation percentage of the private foundation for the fiscal period by the fair market value of all issued and outstanding shares in that class at the end of the fiscal period
Private foundation not disclosing a material transaction in a class of shares at the end of its fiscal period when disclosure is required	10% of the result of multiplying the divestment obligation percentage of the private foundation in that class of shares by the fair market value of all issued and outstanding shares in that class for the fiscal period	10% of the result of multiplying the divestment obligation percentage of the private foundation in that class of shares by the fair market value of all issued and outstanding shares in that class for the fiscal period

Table 1 – List of Charity Penalties		
Infraction	**Penalty/Suspension for FIRST INFRACTION**	**Penalty/Suspension FOR REPEAT INFRACTIONS**
Private foundation not disclosing a material interest held at the end of its fiscal period, by a relevant person, in a class of shares when disclosure is required	10% of the result of multiplying the divestment obligation percentage of the private foundation in that class of shares by the fair market value of all issued and outstanding shares in that class for the fiscal period	10% of the result of multiplying the divestment obligation percentage of the private foundation in that class of shares by the fair market value of all issued and outstanding shares in that class for the fiscal period
Private foundation not disclosing its total corporate holdings percentage at the end of its fiscal period in a class of shares when disclosure is required	10% of the result of multiplying the divestment obligation percentage of the private foundation in that class of shares by the fair market value of all issued and outstanding shares in that class for the fiscal period	10% of the result of multiplying the divestment obligation percentage of the private foundation in that class of shares by the fair market value of all issued and outstanding shares in that class for the fiscal period
Gifts other than *designated gifts* received from a non-arm's length charity that are not spent by the recipient charity on its own charitable activities or transferred to an arm's length qualified donee in the current or following tax year – this amount is in addition to a charity's *disbursement quota*	For the recipient charity, a penalty of 110% of the amount not expended or gifted	For the recipient charity, a penalty of 110% of the amount not expended or gifted

Table 1 – List of Charity Penalties

Infraction	Penalty/Suspension for FIRST INFRACTION	Penalty/Suspension FOR REPEAT INFRACTIONS
Carrying out partisan political activities, or political activities that are not connected and subordinate to the charity's charitable purposes or carrying on political activities when the charity is not devoting substantially all its resources to charitable activities and purposes	One-year suspension of tax-receipting privileges	One-year suspension of tax-receipting privileges
Providing incomplete or inaccurate information on the annual information return (Form T3010)	Suspension of tax-receipting privileges until the required information is provided to the CRA on Form T3010	Suspension of tax-receipting privileges until the required information is provided to the CRA on Form T3010

The range of sanctions up to and including suspension are considered intermediate sanctions. However, despite Parliament's intention to give the CRA additional tools, the CRA effectively restricts itself to compliance agreements and revocation and very few intermediate sanctions have been levied since the sanctions were initially legislated in 2001. This effectively means that for charities facing potential sanction, the best case scenario would be a compliance agreement. The worst case scenario is generally revocation. For this reason it is important to understand the circumstances by which the Charities Directorate decides to implement one punishment over another as described below.

As an aside, CRA auditors often discover tax compliance errors which do not really fall within the scope of a review of the organization's charitable activities. This generally involves the issuance of T4 forms and other employee issues. It is not uncommon for the Charities Directorate to raise revocation as a punishment for these types of offences. Charities should know that the CRA cannot revoke for such an offense.

PENALTY GUIDELINES

Given the range of punishments and the Charities Directorate's unfortunate reluctance to use the intermediate sanction tools given to them by Parliament, the Directorate has developed a continuum by which it decides when the offence is so severe that it will pursue revocation rather than a compliance agreement. This document is available at **www.runningacharity.ca** and is called "Guidelines for Applying Sanctions."

The CRA's first step is to analyze the charity's non-compliance to determine the severity of the offence. The criteria which the CRA takes into account will include whether the charity has been warned before, the amount of money at stake, whether the activity involved was a tax shelter/criminal/terrorist activity, and whether it can be legitimately be said that the charity knew better.

Added to the concerns the Directorate lists in their guidelines, are certain matters which are unstated. In our experience, the CRA will also make a subjective analysis about the type of organization facing revocation. Certain larger charitable organizations, while not untouchable, are of a type that their revocation would pose great difficulties for the Charities Directorate from a political perspective - for example, universities and hospitals. We are unsure of how the Directorate may make this analysis but it does seem clear that the Directorate will take a softer hand for certain organizations that may otherwise face revocation.

Depending on the Directorate's analysis of the appropriate punishment it may levy one of a number of penalties. The most basic response to an audit is what the CRA calls an education letter. These letters are relatively rare but effectively offer advice to the charity in terms of its compliance and ensuring that the charity remains onside of the rules. The next most severe punishment are compliance agreements (described in greater detail in the next section) which effectively force the charity to agree that it is not in compliance and will be in compliance in the future. If a later audit determines that the organization is still not in compliance the Directorate may then decide to pursue revocation as the charity has been warned once.

In theory, the CRA may decide to pursue an intermediate sanction which could include a financial penalty or suspension of the charity's status but these penalties are effectively ignored by the Directorate. The final, and most serious, punishment is revocation. (Annulment of a charity is also a possibility but it is only used where the charity was either improperly registered in the first place or the law has changed such that the charity no longer qualifies for registered status. We do not consider this an intermediate sanction because it is not a punishment for something the charity has done wrong rather it is a mechanism which is necessary to deal with changes in the law.)

COMPLIANCE AGREEMENTS

As stated earlier, charities are often left hoping for a compliance agreement as opposed to the more serious sanction of revocation, nevertheless charities should be wary of signing them. Firstly, compliance agreements generally require the charity to admit fault. This admission can, and will, be used against the charity in any future decision by the CRA to revoke the organization's status based on the same offence. Second, this admission of guilt could be used by the CRA as justification to assess the donors to the charity if the admission relates to their donations. We have seen such situations where the charity signs a compliance agreement because it is the best alternative for the charity but then suffer public relations disasters because the CRA insists on assessing all the donors as a result. The charity is then in the unfortunate position of having to explain to the donors why the CRA refused to change its mind given that the charity had already agreed that the donations were improperly receipted.

Furthermore, just because the "punishment" being offered is not revocation does not necessarily mean that the Charities Directorate is correct in its position that the charity was offside the rules in the first place. We have seen other situations where the Directorate has proposed a compliance agreement for circumstances in which there is a great deal of doubt that the charity did anything wrong. Unfortunately, if the charity does not sign the compliance agreement it is left to the CRA to decide whether or not to pursue revocation. Should the CRA pursue revocation then the charity is immediately forced into the appeal process described below. The appeal process itself can be a punishment given the cost and resources which would have to be dedicated by the charity to defending itself.

Charities are therefore often in a difficult position in deciding whether to sign the compliance agreement, thereby admitting fault but avoiding the difficulties of defending itself and the additional public relations problems which result from admitting offence. That said, there is room for negotiation on the terms of the agreement. The CRA will obviously not change the substance of the agreement, but there may be some room to negotiate the wording around the admission of guilt by the charity. Even though such agreements are not supposed to become public there are circumstances where they can, and changes to the wording can have important consequences. Under these circumstances, organizations that are facing compliance agreements should consult with experienced legal counsel to determine whether it is appropriate to sign such agreements and the consequences which might follow.

OBJECTIONS

If the CRA decides to proceed with revocation, the charity can expect to receive a letter entitled *Notice of Intent to Revoke*. The Notice of Intent to Revoke begins the revocation period known as the "winding up period" discussed elsewhere in this book. An organization that wishes to avoid revocation must file a *Notice of Objection* to the Charities Redress Section at this address:

Tax and Charities Appeals Directorate
Appeals Branch
Canada Revenue Agency
250 Albert Street
Ottawa, ON K1A 0L5

The same approach would be followed by a charity which received a *Notice of Refusal to Register*. An organization that is revoked for failure to file the annual T3010 return would generally not follow this approach but would rather file a new application for charity status along with the T3010 along with a $500 filing penalty fee.

The Charities Redress Section is typically staffed with people who have some level of seniority and have an understanding of the context and laws under which a charity operates. Their mandate is to ensure that the Charities Directorate has applied its mandate correctly. For this reason a charity cannot necessarily expect that the case will have a different disposition at the redress section. Rather, the question to the redress section will simply be whether the particular officer at the Directorate level has properly applied the law. It may be that not all the facts were presented to the original level and so this is an opportunity to further illuminate the file for the purpose of the redress section officer (and sometimes in preparation for an inevitable court hearing). Another possibility may be that the Directorate improperly revoked it because the severity of the infraction was not of a type that should elicit revocation based on a determination of the *Guideline for Intermediate Sanctions*.

Fundamentally, an appeal to the Redress Section should not be considered another "kick at the can." The Redress Section is a check of the actions of the Directorate and only if there is room to argue that the decision was improperly made, can there be some expectation of success at the Redress Section.

Once a *Notice of Intent to Revoke* is received, the charity has ninety days to file its *Notice of Objection*. The Redress Section is much smaller than the Directorate and as it currently stands, it generally seems unable to deal with the volume of objections in a timely fashion. A charity can expect a significant delay between filing a Notice of Objection to the time when an officer is assigned to the case. It is not unheard of for the delay to exceed one year. During this time the organization is in the winding up period described in Chapter 10.

The revocation process is not complete until the CRA publishes the final Notice of Revocation in the Canada Gazette. Technically this revocation can be finalized as soon as thirty days after the Notice of Intent to Revoke is sent. Typically such quick action is reserved for organizations involved in tax shelters and what the CRA terms to be aggravated non-compliance.

The Court, on the other hand, applies a somewhat different test to determine whether immediate revocation is appropriate. That test involves an examination into the harm caused by an immediate revocation (rather than waiting for the charity's appeals regarding the CRA's reasons for revocation to be heard) and whether that harm can be remedied through the payment of money (although there are other parts of this test as well). Sometimes charities are in the frustrating position of having lost their charitable status while still waiting to hear from the Redress Section as to the merits and demerits of revocation. Unfortunately, the law allows such a situation.

If, after filing a Notice of Objection, the delay at the Charities Redress Section exceeds 90 days, the charity can skip the rest of the wait and file its *Notice of Appeal* at the Federal Court of Appeal. Of course, this means that if the charity had a viable case at the Redress Section it misses the opportunity to resolve the matter at that level and avoid the legal fees associated with an appeal to the courts.

As described in the Chapter 10 section on revocation tax, a revoked charity could become liable for what is known as the revocation tax. Under certain circumstances a charity may receive a *Notice of Assessment for Revocation Tax* from the CRA indicating that the (now revoked) charity owes some amount of revocation tax. If the organization wishes to object to the Notice of Assessment it will file a *Notice of Objection* to the revocation tax to the Charities Redress Section at the address already provided. The content of such a Notice of Objection would include, besides the name and address and business number of the charity, the actual circumstances for the proper calculation of the Revocation Tax. Under most circumstances it will also include a filing of the T2046 if it was not done previously.

If there is a dispute over what is properly included in the revocation tax - an appeal from a decision from the Charities Redress Section in relation to the revocation tax will go to the Tax Court of Canada rather than the Federal Court of Appeal. In both cases a knowledgeable tax litigation lawyer should be retained to resolve the matter.

APPEALS

Charities which receive an unfavorable result from their appeal to the Charities Redress Section may consider an appeal to the Federal Court of Appeal or for appeals of Revocation Tax to the Tax Court of Canada. At the Federal Court of Appeal an incorporated entity cannot be represented must be represented by legal counsel. Appeals to the Federal Court of Appeal must be approached seriously and it would be unlikely that an organization could be successful without retaining qualified legal counsel immediately upon learning it must file to the court. The same is true of appeals to the Tax Court of Canada.

8

Spending Money

In any country where the government subsidizes donations it should not be surprising that strict legislative restrictions are in place on the spending of those donations; Canada is no different. However, Parliament's efforts in this are hindered by the fact that the constitutional power to regulate charities lies with the provinces. The Federal Government is (at least technically) restricted to legislation that is reasonably related to the implementation of an income tax. And one could argue – although it has not been done yet – that details of spending by charities would therefore be beyond the jurisdiction of the Federal Government. Nevertheless, the *Income Tax Act* contains a variety of provisions which effectively ignore this limitation and which have been expanded upon over time by the CRA and the Courts. This chapter is will review those restrictions and provide an outline by which organizations can guide themselves in spending their charitable funds.

DISBURSEMENT QUOTA

Paragraph 149.1(1) of the Income Tax Act defines a charitable organization as:

> " . . . at any particular time, means an organization, whether or not incorporated, all the resources of which are devoted to charitable activities carried on by the organization itself . . . "

Read on its face, this would seem to mean that a charitable organization (i.e. not a foundation) can only use its assets and resources in pursuit of its charitable objects. While generally the law is to be read as simply as possible, in this case the law was never understood to mean exactly as it would seem. Instead charities have always been allowed to conduct administrative activities necessary for their general operation even if this would seemingly violate the principle that charitable organizations must devote all of their resources to the pursuit of their own charitable activities. This includes everything from fundraising to hiring staff and the use of professional advisors incidental to running a functioning organization.

When the law was originally drafted in the 1970's it was understood that there would need to be some sort of relieving provision to allow charities to spend some amount of their resources on non-charitable activities. This provision was originally intended to be the disbursement quota (DQ). The actual DQ formula began simply and evolved into a creature with five variables and various definitions unintelligible to practically everyone. Fortunately, the formula was recently simplified as follows:

"Disbursement quota," for a taxation year of a registered charity, means the amount determined by the formula -

$$A \times B \times 0.035/365$$

where,
A is the number of days in the taxation year, and B is
(a) the prescribed amount for the year, in respect of all or a portion of a property owned by the charity at any time in the 24 months immediately preceding the taxation year that was not used directly in charitable activities or administration, if that amount is greater than

(A) if the registered charity is a charitable organization, $100,000, and

(B) in any other case, $25,000, and

(C) in any other case, nil.

Understanding this definition can be further simplified.

Generally, variable "A" will be 365 (days). It would be shorter in a year in which the charity begins or terminates its operations. (And in a leap year it is 366). Variable "B" refers to a "prescribed amount." The prescribed amount is defined in the Regulations to the Income Tax Act and can be easily changed by the bureaucracy (although this has not happened since the disbursement quota provisions were amended in the 2000's). The prescription for variable "B" is rather complicated but we have nevertheless reproduced it below.

Regulation 3701

(1) For the purposes of the description of B in the definition "disbursement quota" in subsection 149.1(1) of the Act, the prescribed amount for a taxation year of a registered charity is determined as follows:

(a) choose a number, not less than two and not more than eight, of equal and consecutive periods that total twenty-four months and that end immediately before the beginning of the year;

(b) aggregate for each period chosen under paragraph (*a*) all amounts, each of which is the value, determined in accordance with section 3702, of a property, or a portion of a property, owned by the registered charity, and not used directly in charitable activities or administration, on the last day of the period;

(c) aggregate all amounts, each of which is the aggregate of values determined for each period under paragraph (*b*); and

(d) divide the aggregate amount determined under paragraph (*c*) by the number of periods chosen under paragraph (*a*).

(2) For the purposes of subsection (1) and subject to subsection (3)

(a) The number of periods chosen under paragraph (1)(a) may be changed by the registered charity for its first taxation year commencing after 1986 and the new number shall, unless otherwise authorized by the Minister, be used for that taxation year and all subsequent taxation years.

(b) a registered charity is deemed to have existed on the last day of each of the periods chosen by it.

(3) The number of periods chosen under paragraph (1)(*a*) may be changed by the registered charity for its first taxation year commencing after 1986 and the new number shall, unless otherwise authorized by the Minister, be used for that taxation year and all subsequent taxation years.

DETERMINATION OF VALUE

Regulation 3702.

(1) For the purposes of subsection 3701(1), the value of a property, or a portion of a property, owned by a registered charity, and not used directly in charitable activities or administration, on the last day of a period is determined as of that day to be -

(a) in the case of a non-qualified investment of a private foundation, the greater of its fair market value on that day and its cost amount to the private foundation;

(b) subject to paragraph (c), in the case of property other than a non-qualified investment that is
(i) a share of a corporation that is listed on a designated stock exchange, the closing price or the average of the bid and asked prices of that share on that day or, if there is no closing price or bid and asked prices on that day, on the last preceding day for which there was a closing price or bid and asked prices,

(ii) a share of a corporation that is not listed on a designated stock exchange, the fair market value of that share on that day,

(iii) an interest in real property or a real right in an immovable, the fair market value on that day of the interest or right less the amount of any debt of the registered charity incurred in respect of the acquisition of the interest or right and secured by the interest or right, where the debt bears a reasonable rate of interest,

(iv) a contribution that is the subject of a pledge, nil,

(v) an interest, or for civil law a right, in property where the registered charity does not have the present use or enjoyment of the interest or right, nil,

(vi) a life insurance policy, other than an annuity contract, that has not matured, nil, and

(vii) a property not described in any of subparagraphs (i) to (vi), the fair market value of the property on that day; and

(c) in the case of any property described in paragraph (b) that is owned in connection with the charitable activities of the registered charity and is a share of a limited-dividend housing company referred to in paragraph 149(1)(n) of the Act or a loan, that has ceased to be used for charitable purposes and is being held pending disposition or for use in charitable activities, or that has been acquired for use in charitable activities, the lesser of the fair market value of the property on that day and an amount determined by the formula

$$(A / 0.035) \times (12 / B)$$

Where A is the income earned on the property in the period, and B is the number of months in the period.

(2) For the purposes of subsection (1), a method that the Minister may accept for the determination of the fair market value of property or a portion thereof on the last day of a period is an independent appraisal made

(a) in the case of property described in subparagraph (1)(b)(ii) or (iii), not more than three years before that day; and

(b) in the case of property described in paragraph (1)(a), subparagraph (1)(b)(vii) or paragraph (1)(c), not more than one year before that day.

As the DQ, at this point, is intended to force charities to spend a percentage of their assets not used directly in charitable activities in the previous 24 months, it is important to assign a value to those assets which qualify. These provisions, as complicated as they are, effectively allow a charity to average out the value of those assets so that it can complete the calculation. Such averaging provisions are clearly required when one considers that the value of a stock portfolio is in constant flux. Once this averaging is completed, the application of the rest of the formula is relatively clear.

Assets not used in charitable activities are typically endowments (generally cash) that are invested so that the charity may benefit from the income earned on the amounts. At times, a charity may attract donations greater than that required for its operational use and so it forms the corpus of an investment portfolio for the future benefit of the organization. For example, an organization with an endowment of $100,000 in 2014 would be obligated to spend 3.5% of that amount in the year 2015. This would mean that the organization should aim to earn at least 3.5% on its principal so that it can meet its quota in 2015.

Organizations that transfer funds from themselves to another organization and then have spending done by the other organization do not benefit from a double dip in the amount of the disbursement quota. At least one of the organizations must spend the money on charitable activities. Nevertheless there may be a one-year deferral depending on the circumstances of the transfer.

There are a couple of important notes to make about the DQ. First, the DQ always acts one-year in arrears. For example, the spending requirement in year two depends on the assets not used in charitable activity in year one. Second, with the exception of the minimum threshold levels, the disbursement quota affects private foundations, public foundations and charitable foundations in the same way. Third, charities that are planning to undertake large capital expenditures may be building up a large amount of capital in order to purchase something - for example, a building. If that is the case, the charity should contact the CRA to request an exemption for the calculation of the DQ. To do so a letter with the following information should be sent to the address below.

- the specific purpose for which the funds will be used
- the amount required
- the length of time needed to accumulate the funds (minimum 3 years and maximum 10 years)
- the signature of a director/trustee or other authorized representative of the charity
- the name and the registration number of the charity
- the effective date (starting date)

Mail or fax the letter to:

Charities Directorate
Canada Revenue Agency
Ottawa ON
K1A 0L5

Finally, sometimes, in circumstances beyond the control of the charity, it may be unable to meet its DQ. This may happen in cases of theft from the charity, or simply a dramatic financial downturn (such as happened in 2008). In these cases the charity may ask the CRA to consider a DQ reduction. Such a reduction will only be considered if the charity has already applied any available DQ excess against the year from either previous or later years. To request a reduction the charity must complete form T2094 (available on **www.runningacharity.ca**).

FUNDRAISING EXPENSES

As stated in the introduction, the constitutional authority of the Federal Government in legislating regulations for charities is, in fact, limited. This is implicitly recognized in the document put out by the CRA documenting its expectations for fundraising. It is entitled *Fundraising by Registered Charities* available on **www.runningacharity.ca**.

The fact remains, however, that fundraising expenses *is* an issue of tremendous concern to the public. Consequently, the CRA has assumed the role of regulator of charities in the public interest and has provided guidance on appropriate fundraising expenses. Even if there is no particular legal provision on which the CRA could rely upon to revoke a charity specifically for extraordinarily high fundraising expenses, there are numerous other provisions on which the CRA could build a case for revocation on the same facts.

The guidance uses the same basic definition of "fundraising" as one would imagine. Effectively, it is solicitation of any type of donation. There are a number of comments to make on the nature of fundraising but they should be common sense to most organizations. Clearly, charities cannot engage in deceptive or illegal activity to fundraise (although this is not an income tax rule). Neither can they make fundraising their primary activity. Some charities run into problems when they use third-party fundraisers that bill the charity for their services. In these cases, where the CRA finds the expenses paid objectionable, they will make the argument that the charity now exists to benefit these third parties rather than to pursue their own charitable objects. So, charities hiring third-party fundraisers should be careful about their arrangements.

Appropriate fundraising expenses are calculated as a percentage of revenue in the year. It is a fairly easy calculation as all fundraising expenses (including appropriate allocations of staff time and office resources) are divided by the charity's total fundraising revenue in the year. Fundraising revenue includes both receipted and unreceipted donations but is not limited to revenue raised directly as a result of a specific fundraising activity. Effectively, calculating in this way averages out the fundraising expenses for a specific campaign over all of the revenue raised by all fundraising campaigns. Clearly, this benefits organizations with already large fundraising efforts and allows them to spend a greater percentage of revenue on starting a specific campaign then would a smaller group. Recognizing this, the CRA does try to make allowances for charities with less than $100,000 in revenue.

Fundraising expenses are divided into three bands: 35% and under, 36% to 70% and over 70%. The first band of fundraising expenses is unlikely to raise concerns from the CRA. That being said though, should the expenses consistently be at a level of 35% one would imagine that the CRA will take a closer look at the necessity of the organization for incurring consistently high fundraising expenses (this would be in addition to its other administrative expenses).

The second band of fundraising expenses would raise concerns at the CRA and the charity would have to explain why its ratio is so high (of course the higher the ratio, the better the explanation would have to be). For example, in some circumstances an organization may be undertaking some sort of acquisition campaign to seek new donors and for a limited period of time may have rather high fundraising expenses. If that is the case, the CRA would look for decreasing expenses in time as the organization's revenue increases.

Fundraising expenses in excess of 70% of an organization's revenue will be considered inappropriate. Again while the CRA cannot technically revoke for excessive fundraising expenses one can confidently predict that the CRA will find some other grounds on which to revoke such an organization. It should also be noted though that the CRA is not completely oblivious to the situations in which charities operate and are generally approachable when explaining extenuating circumstances which lead to higher than anticipated fundraising expenses.

Regardless of the CRA's position on fundraising expenses and its constitutional authority, the fact remains that the public is exceedingly interested in the administrative expenses of charities. Any charity with excessively high fundraising expenses is undertaking a risk.

DEALS WITH BOARD MEMBERS

As a rule, charities try to collect board members from different walks of life. This is generally because charities can benefit from the varied experiences of those around the table. Periodically, directors have access to goods or services that the charity may require. This is often true of lawyers and accountants, but it is equally true of painters, electricians and businessmen.

Because the directors are typically in a position to know what the charity needs, they are tempted to provide their goods or services to the charity. Often these people provide the goods and services at a cost less than fair market value. These transactions are generally prohibited by common law as directors have a duty not to benefit from the assets of the charity. This includes <u>any benefit</u> and not simply a duty not to be paid in their role as director. Consequently directors are generally forbidden from selling their goods or services to the charity for any amount.

If a charity and the director agree that they require this particular service from the director the charity may get approval from a court to engage in this transaction. Only Ontario has a procedure which makes such a rare request routine.[7] In other

7 See the Public Guardian and Trustee for more information

provinces the courts may not even have any idea that they have this authority and it is consequently difficult to get such approvals. Under the common law a director who benefits from a charity's property in this way could be forced to repay every penny that was billed to the charity. (It is our understanding that this has never happened in Canada but then again, nobody wants to be the first!)

From an income tax perspective, the CRA's jurisdiction extends to such situations where a director or member of the charity receives a benefit to which they were not due. This involves either a payment in excess of fair market value of goods and services provided or where the charity foregoes receiving income to which it would be entitled, to the benefit of a director or member.

This provision effectively allows the CRA to punish the charity for bestowing the undue benefit whereas the common law is intended to punish the director. This of course, assumes that the charity had the legal authority in the first place to engage in a business relationship with the director.

MAINTAINING CONTROL AND DIRECTION

As discussed previously, the definition of a "charitable organization" is one where the organization conducts its own charitable activities. This implies that a charity is *restricted* to dedicating its resources to carrying out its own charitable activities. Carrying out one's own charitable activities is understood to require the charity to maintain control and direction over its resources as those activities are conducted. Where the charity is actually the one conducting its activities this is not a problem. For example, a charity whose volunteers are operating a soup kitchen will clearly have control over its resources. Similarly an organization which sends volunteers to conduct operations abroad would appear to have control and direction over the resources being used to implement those activities.[8]

However, the situation becomes more difficult where a charity is working with a partner. For example, a "Canadian friends of" organization that works to help people in a foreign jurisdiction. In this example, the organization may not actually send volunteers to implement the activities and may work with a group or organization in that country. Maintaining control and direction over the spending of funds is the fundamental requirement of an organization which is operating locally or abroad. The test for control and direction does not apply simply to an organization's actual cash but also to the goods purchased with those funds.

Control and direction effectively means that decisions over the charity's resources are made by the charity itself. This must be the case whether the charity operates only in Canada or elsewhere as well. While applying the test may vary

8 Obviously, transfers to other qualified donees are allowed.

in different circumstances, the overall effect is the same and charities must ask themselves whether they have outsourced the decision-making over their resources to others (unacceptable) or are listening to the advice of others and making their own decision (acceptable). Indicators to consider would include what would happen if the charity decided to pull out of the specific project. Could the charity receive back any goods or property it has purchased? Would it be able to identify which items are theirs and which are not? And could it determine that all of its resources to date have only been used to pursue its charitable purposes? These are all questions that CRA auditors will ask if brought in to review the situation.

Many Canadian charities operate overseas with foreign partners. Where the Canadian charity sends funds abroad it must ensure that it maintains control and direction over those funds – and any property purchased with those resources. To make matters somewhat more difficult, CRA auditors can only judge control and direction if proper documentation is kept.

When an auditor looks at a charity he or she seeks to find evidence that the funds of the charity were never used for non-charitable purposes and that they *could* never have been used without the charity's explicit authorization. The organization must show not only that the funds *could not* have been spent on non-charitable activities but in fact *were not* spent on non-charitable activities. The CRA recommends that when carrying out activities through an intermediary, the following steps are undertaken:

a. Create a written agreement with the intermediary, and implement its terms.
b. Communicate a clear, complete and detailed description of the activity to the intermediary.
c. Monitor and supervise the activity.
d. Provide clear, complete and detailed instructions to the intermediary on an ongoing basis.
e. Arrange for the intermediary to keep the charity's funds separate from its own, and to keep separate books and records.
f. Make periodic transfers of resources, based on demonstrated performance.

The evidence that a charity may use to prove it has control and direction over its resources will vary with the circumstances. Clearly where the transfer of funds is involved it will necessitate banking documents, including a separate bank account and copies of foreign exchange receipts as well as any other financial documents showing the transfer of funds and the spending of those funds abroad. However, it may also involve diaries, video evidence, statements by volunteers investigating the spending of funds abroad and thank you letters from beneficiaries of the charitable funds. All of these can be used to show that the charity has been maintaining control and direction over the funds as they travel from Canada for spending on travel expenses abroad.

There are four ways in which a charity may consider spending its funds on its charitable activities. The first and most obvious is where the charity conducts its activities by itself. The second is where the charity purchases goods and services by way of contract from a third party, such as purchasing mosquito nets rather than making nets themselves. The third and perhaps most popular way involves an *Agency Agreement* and the final way involves acting in a joint venture with a group of other partners.

OPERATING THROUGH AN AGENT

In an agency relationship there are generally two parties, the principal and the agent. The agent operates as an arm of the principal in the sense that it cannot do anything without the express permission and direction of the principal. (On the flip side, if the agent is sued for an activity conducted on behalf of the principal the principal will also be liable.) These relationships should be established by an *Agency Agreement* between the parties. A sample *Agency Agreement* can be found at **www.runningacharity.ca**.

Typically, the CRA will require an *Agency Agreement* where the agent is not paid for its role in acting as such. As a result, the agents are typically organizations or people already invested in the outcome which the charity seeks to influence.

A detailed agency agreement should be constructed and followed to the letter. Generally, such agreements allow the agent to suggest to the principal some method by which charitable objectives may be furthered. The charity would then consider the suggestion and if it decides to proceed, it would have internal documentation approving the suggestion. The charity would then transfer a portion of the funds (if sensible in the circumstances) to a bank account upon which the agent has signing authority. This (generally foreign) account would only contain the funds belonging to the principal. The agent would, as part of its suggestion, have provided a potential budget for use in the proposed project. The charity would expect proof that the funds had been spent on the items included in the proposed budget. If this has been established, then the charity may authorize the allocation of a second tranche of funds. The process would continue until the project was finished, if ever.

Where the project involves the purchase of assets or real estate, the principal would be expected to exert control and direction over those assets through the agent. This would involve identifying the assets in such a way that they are known to belong to the Canadian charity and ensuring that they are only used for charitable purposes. Inherent in this assurance is knowledge by the charity regarding the purposes for which they are being used and the ability to withdraw the resources if they are no longer going to be used for charitable purposes. Ideally, it would also require permission by the charity over their use in a particular circumstance but of course such an arrangement can be difficult to enforce long-distance.

The agency relationship can be administratively difficult in the sense that there must be a great deal of paperwork that is passed from the agent to the principal. To make matters worse, the CRA expects the charity to maintain original documentation in either English or French. Regardless of the administrative difficulties, the agency relationship is the easiest way in which a charity can maintain control and direction over situations in which it operates in a different locality. Where operating via an agency agreement, or perhaps ownership of property in a foreign country is contrary to the local law, the CRA may be consulted for acceptable alternatives.

OPERATING THROUGH A JOINT VENTURE

Many Canadian organizations have sister groups in other countries. For example, religious groups will often have co-religionists who have established operations in places like the United States, Europe, the Middle East, or Asia. Those groups may wish to undertake a charitable activity together in some foreign country such as the example of Catholics in Canada, the United States and the Netherlands working together to build a school in Africa. In these circumstances, an Agency agreement may be inappropriate because it typically involves the agent operating by itself under the direction of the Canadian principal whereas working with sister groups would clearly contradict this principle.

In these circumstances the CRA is prepared to accept organizations operating as part of a joint venture. A joint venture exists where different parties all contribute something to the overall project. In these circumstances, the Charities Directorate expects the organization to maintain control and direction over the overall project in proportion to the resources it contributes. For example, in a $1,000,000 project, if a Canadian charity was contributing 30% the CRA would expect the organization to have 30% representation on the board of management for the project.

In a joint venture relationship it can often be hard to show control and direction even with some seat on management. Clearly if the Canadian charity is only a minority participant it will not be able to call the shots on how the project is developed. The recognition by the CRA of a joint venture is *de facto* recognition of the practical principal that Canadian charities do not operate in a vacuum and they often operate with partner organizations abroad. Notwithstanding this recognition of the facts on the ground, a Canadian charity would be well-advised to ensure that whatever project it engages in is in pursuit of its charitable objects and can only be used to pursue those objects.

PURCHASING FROM AN OVERSEAS SUPPLIER

Clearly, the CRA is concerned with how a charity spends its resources. Spending within Canada is fairly easy to document because Canadian financial transactions are sophisticated enough that it would be expected that the organization would be able to show the receipts for goods or services spent and can generally show financial transactions from beginning to end.

The same is not necessarily true in foreign jurisdictions. To begin with, receipts are not necessarily standard business practice around the world. Moreover, those receipts would not necessarily be in English or French. Furthermore, in certain countries cancelled cheques are not made available by banks and in others purchases by cash are the norm. In all of these circumstances, the charity will still be expected to provide documentary evidence that the money has been used to purchase resources to further the organization's charitable purposes.

Obviously, the ability to prove this spending is dependent on the documents that the charity can obtain from the source. However, even where the charity is unable to maintain standard business documentation, it may be possible to collect the necessary documentary evidence. For example, photographs of the purchased material may be sufficient in the circumstances. Similarly it may be possible to prove the purchase and distribution of certain materials if there is photographic evidence of the final product. For example, the purchase of building materials may be evident in the construction of a final product. In these circumstances, the CRA may be able to accept the fact that a building exists as proof that purchases of building materials were also made. One would also likely require evidence of local prices for such materials.

Operating abroad can be fraught with administrative difficulties for charities but generally once the organization understands the local milieu in which it is operating, the ability to provide the necessary evidence increases as well.

INTERNATIONAL BRANCHES OF THE SAME ORGANIZATION

Being a country of immigrants, Canada is an inviting place for international organizations to set up domestic branches. Such groups often require the Canadian branch to pay "dues" to the international parent body. However, there are strict limitations on the ability of Canadian organizations to help fund the global operations of the groups in which it participates. This is often not understood by the foreign (usually American) "parent" which can expect the Canadian organization to pay up some percentage of its revenue as dues to the global operation.

The CRA's general policy in this regard is that the organization may pay 5% of the charity's expenses in the year, or $5000 - whichever is the lesser. Often, both the Canadian and foreign organization find this situation highly unsatisfactory.

The relationship between the Canadian and international group is usually one of mutual benefit. The international organization often provides guidance and support, (if not actual resources) for use in the Canadian branch's operations. Even if the parent organization does not charge for these resources, it may be worthwhile for the Canadian organization to consider paying for them. While the Canadian organization is restricted to paying no more than fair market value for the assets transferred to it, this is one way the Canadian organization may consider sending money back to the parent organization in a way that meets the expectations of both the parent body and the CRA.

Arrangements such as this are complicated and require a valuation of the goods and services coming to the Canadian organization. This valuation should be done by a trained professional so as to assure the CRA that no more than fair market value is being spent on the goods and services coming back to the Canadian organization from the charity's foreign parent (or any other party).

9

GST-HST Issues

For most charities the issue of GST/HST is one-sided, that is, it is an issue of paying the tax rather than collecting it. However, charities can be required to collect the GST/HST just as any other organization. The GST/HST issues for charities are particularly complicated, even in comparison to the other rules that guide charities, so unless an organization has exceedingly simple financial transactions it should consult an experienced professional regarding the organization's GST/HST obligations. This chapter is intended to outline some of the more salient features of the GST/HST regime in the hopes that they can guide people into asking the appropriate questions.

Structure of the Act

The GST/HST is the tax levied on products sold. It is intended to be borne by the final consumer of the particular product. Consumers pay tax on the things that they buy. If they in turn sell the item either together or refashion it as some other item, they generally charge tax on the product sold. Then, that consumer (now producer) remits to the government the total of the tax on the item charged, less the tax paid on the inputs.

The end consumer pays the tax on the product purchased but cannot claim any credits from the government. The credit for tax paid on inputs is called the *Input Tax Credit*.

Example:

If Simcha purchases fabric from a fabric store he will have to pay the proper GST/HST rate for that province. If he uses that fabric to make a suit for himself then he pays the final tax. If, on the other hand, Simcha produces a suit *for sale* he will collect the proper GST/HST from his customer, deduct from that the amount that he paid to his supplier, and remit the difference to the government. In this way the "burden" of the tax lies with the penultimate consumer of the product.

Some items are exempt from tax. This means that the consumer does not pay any tax on the item purchased. However, the seller of an exempt product (called an exempt supply) is not entitled to any *Input Tax Credits* on the item sold. This contrasts with items that are called *zero rated*. These items in fact have a tax rate of 0% (i.e. there is no charge). This entitles the seller of a zero rated supply to an *Input Tax Credit* of a normal amount. Items which qualify for either treatment are listed in the *Excise Tax Act*. Given that many charities sell or produce exempt supplies, Parliament has included a mechanism by which these organizations can receive a rebate (rather than a refund) of a portion of the tax paid. In other words, registered charities can receive back 50% of the GST / HST they pay regardless of whether the tax is paid on inputs to produce other products. This is effectively a gift to charities to help offset the tax burden they would otherwise shoulder. As we are speaking specifically of charities, our discussion below is limited to the rebate applicable to these organizations.

Where a charity is engaged in the sale of items which are neither exempt nor zero rated and at a sufficient level, the organization may be required to register for a GST/HST number. If the charity does register for such a number then they are required to charge tax for the items sold (which are neither exempt nor zero rated). Organizations which do sell taxable items may not claim the 100% input tax credits unless they are registered.

The Federal government charges GST at 5%. Various Provincial governments add their percentage of tax on top of the 5% federal portion. In those provinces in which there is a provincial component, the GST is referred to as the Harmonized Sales Tax i.e. the HST. For the most part, the application of the law is the same to all provinces with the obvious exception of the rates which are charged. However, there are certain differences. The most important of these for the purposes of this discussion relate to the amount of rebate to which different charities are entitled. This is outlined later in the chapter.

EXEMPT SUPPLIES

As described previously, exempt supplies are those for which there is no tax to be paid. And unlike zero rated supplies there are no input tax credits available for those inputs required to produce such goods. The list of exempt supplies is included within the *Excise Tax Act* and includes most of those items which we have come to expect to be provided by charities.

Some property and services are exempt regardless of who supplies them. For example, childcare services (defined as the primary purpose of which is to provide care and supervision of children 14 years of age and under for periods of less than 24 hours per day) are exempt. Other goods and services are exempt if they are provided by a charity, such as catering services for private functions (wedding receptions), meals on wheels programs or the supply of used or donated goods.

There are a variety of examples of items which charities provide and are therefore exempt from GST. These include:

- Admissions to places of amusement such as museums, recreational complexes and theaters if the maximum admission charge is less than a dollar.
- Admissions to anything where part of the admission qualifies for a charitable donation receipt for income tax purposes (see split receipting in Chapter 6).
- Most property or services sold basically at cost.
- Most property and services sold during the course of a fundraising activity unless the property or services is part of a year-long business. Examples include Christmas greeting cards, or chocolate bar drives. It would not include items sold in a year-long gift shop or subscriptions to a charity magazine.
- Membership in a charity unless there are significant financial benefits to membership.
- Supplies of food and beverages or a combination that is provided for purposes of relieving poverty, suffering, or distress of individuals.

Sponsorships

As discussed earlier in this book, sponsorships can be an area in which there is a mixed benefit provided back to the donor. For example, a corporation that provides funding to a charity may be given some form of advertising by the charity to its patrons. From a receipting perspective the value of the advertising returned to the donor must be reflected in a reduced income tax receipt for the donation to the donor.

From a GST/HST perspective, sponsorships may not be subject to tax depending on the nature and extent of the promotional benefits. If the payment by the sponsor is made primarily (more than 50%) to obtain advertising, then the payment will not be considered as sponsorship but rather a payment for advertising services. However, advertising services are generally exempt from GST/HST when provided by a charity. The general question then is whether the organization is engaged in the taxable supply of advertising. If there is any question about this, qualified legal counsel should be retained as the charity may need to be consistently collecting tax on sponsorships.

ZERO RATED SUPPLIES

Zero rated supplies are items for which the tax rate charged on them is 0%, i.e. no tax is actually paid but the seller of those goods can recoup 100% of the tax it paid in producing the item it sold. For this reason, the designation of supplies as zero rated can be relatively beneficial for the supplier. However, the list of supplies is rather small. It typically includes items such as basic groceries, certain goods when they are exported out of Canada, prescription drugs, supplies of blood and blood derivatives, certain medical devices and the rental of farmland.

CHARITIES ELIGIBLE FOR THE GST/HST REBATE

Generally speaking, registered charities are eligible for a rebate of 50% (technically called the *Public Services Bodies* rebate) of the federal part of the tax (i.e. the 5% amount). Organizations eligible to claim this rebate should file form GST 66 called the *Application for GST/HST Public Services Bodies' Rebate* or form GST 284 *Application for GST/HST Public Services Bodies' Rebate* (both forms are available on **www.runningacharity.ca**). Charities are also entitled to a rebate on the provincial portion of the tax in those provinces that participate in the Harmonized Sales Tax. Charities resident in Ontario qualify for 82% rebate of the provincial HST portion, charities in Nova Scotia, New Brunswick, Newfoundland and Labrador qualify for a 50% rebate of their provincial portion and in Prince Edward Island the rate is 35% of the provincial portion.

There may be other rebates available in certain circumstances. A rebate for the purchase of printed books or for other exported property and services are two such examples.

The rebate forms can be filed either electronically using the CRA's online services through GST/HST Netfile or on paper using the form described above. Charities making a filing using either method should also file the appropriate form for the provincial rebate - the *Provincial Schedule Form RC7066SCH, Provincial Schedule –GST/HST Public Services Bodies' Rebate* also available on **www.runningacharity.ca**. As the rebate percentages for the provincial part of the HST are different for the participating provinces, charities will have to separately track the federal and provincial portions of HST paid on their eligible expenses. The charities may wish to consult *Guide RC4034* for instructions on completing the rebate application. Keep in mind that charities are subject to audit by the CRA for their GST matters and therefore must keep necessary documents for six years after the calendar year to which the rebate relates.

REQUIRED REGISTRATION

Most organizations that are engaged in the supply of taxable goods and services will have to register for GST/HST. There are however minimal thresholds of sales that these organizations must meet before they *are required* to register. The threshold tests are below. If these organizations are small suppliers, then they may forego the collection of tax on the goods they sell but this means they are also not entitled to claim input tax credits on the items purchased to produce those goods.

Given that most Canadians are used to paying tax on the items that they purchase, one would imagine that the decision by these charities to not charge tax and not collect the input tax credits is simply based on the administrative difficulty that may exist for organizations in tracking GST/HST in applying for the refund.

GROSS REVENUE TEST

Charities may qualify as a small supplier under either of the:

- $250,000 gross revenue test, or
- $50,000 tax supplies test.

A charity only needs to meet *one* of these tests to be a small supplier.

The gross revenue test is, as it seems, a calculation of the gross revenue of a charity in the fiscal period. The test is calculated on the gross revenue over the previous two fiscal years. In the first fiscal year the charity would not have to register for the GST/HST. In the second year it *must* register if its gross revenue in the first year is more than $250,000. Or, in the third year and ongoing years if the amount is more than $250,000 in either of the two previous years, then it would have to register. Gross revenue includes income from a business, gifts from donations, grants, and property investment income.

$50,000 TAXABLE SUPPLIES TEST

Most supplies produced by a charity are exempt and some are zero rated, however those products or services which are neither exempt nor zero rated are by definition taxable. If the charity is engaged in the sale of taxable supplies and in the last four calendar years, had revenue exceeding $50,000 or in the current quarter will have more than $50,000 the charity will have to register for the collection of tax. This does not include sales of capital property which might attract GST/HST such as the one-time sale of real estate.

If the amounts are $50,000 or less, the organization does not have to register but may choose to do so voluntarily as it would allow the organization to effectively pass the GST/HST onto its final consumers and not shoulder the burden of tax on the inputs it purchases.

ELIGIBLE AND INELIGIBLE EXPENSES

This section relates to the expenses for which a charity can claim the *Public Services Bodies' Rebate* at the applicable rates. The rebate can only be claimed on eligible expenses. Typically, these are expenses for which one cannot claim input tax credits or any other rebate, refund or omission. They include:

- general operating and overhead expenses such as rent, utilities and administration expenses.
- reimbursements paid to employees and volunteers engaged in delivering the activities of the charity. (In other words, items that are paid for by individuals but reimbursed by the charity ostensibly for the purpose of engaging in this business.)
- property and services used, consumed or supplied in producing exempt supplies.
- capital property such as buildings, equipment, medicals, machinery etc used mostly in the delivery of exempt supplies.

Certain expenses are ineligible for the *Public Services Bodies' Rebate*. These types of ineligible expenses include:

- memberships in dining, recreational, sporting clubs.
- property or services acquired primarily for making suppliers of residential accommodation, unless that accommodation is provided to certain individuals in the pursuit of charitable activities.
- property or services acquired to give to an officer, member or employee of the charity unless it falls under a specific type of exemption.

This list is not exhaustive and should be reviewed with qualified legal/financial counsel should the charity find itself filing an application for rebate.

PART III

Death of a Charity

10

Winding Up a Charity

DISSOLUTION: TAX CONSIDERATIONS

Many Canadians who begin a business do not contemplate its possible end. The same is true of the well-meaning individuals who begin charities. Unfortunately, the death of a charity is at least as common as the death of a business. Often, charities shut down because there is simply no one interested in continuing to run them. In other circumstances, the termination of a charity results from the loss of its status as a tax exempt organization with the CRA. But regardless of the reasons for shutdown, the charity (or more practically, the directors) has a number of responsibilities to ensure an orderly windup. Directors must fight the temptation to passively allow an inactive charity to languish if they wish to avoid unnecessary liabilities. A good working knowledge of the rudimentary rules is important to ensure that neither the charity nor its directors are left exposed upon dissolution.

Perhaps the greatest reason to ensure an orderly windup is that under the *Income Tax Act* a deregistered organization must dispose of its assets in satisfaction of the so-called "revocation tax." Another important motivator for orderly dissolution of a charity is that the fiduciary duties that attach to directors may extend indefinitely if the charity is not carefully terminated.

Of course, any dissolving entity may be left with responsibilities under a variety of different laws, including the *Excise Tax Act*, employment legislation, or the various environmental protection acts. Charities may also be subject to laws that pertain specifically to them as a class, such as Ontario's *Religious Organizations*

Lands Act or *Charities Accounting Act*. This chapter will deal primarily with the dissolving charity's responsibilities under the *Income Tax Act*.

CHANGE OF STATUS

As discussed in Chapter 4, an organization is a charity based on whether it has been formed to pursue charitable purposes – regardless of whether or not it is registered as a charity with the CRA. However, registration as a charity clearly has a number of tax advantages and so is pursued by most charities in Canada. The disadvantage of registration is the requirement to abide by the rules imposed on such charities; including those that apply to charitable property should the charity have its registered status revoked.

A registered charity generally loses its status in one of three ways: it can voluntarily seek to have its status revoked; it can be revoked for failure to file its annual return; or it can be revoked for "serious" non-compliance. According to the CRA, serious non-compliance involves an evaluation of the relative monetary size of the infraction, its criminality, breaches of "major" provisions of the Act, or a breach of a previous compliance agreement.

PROCESS

Regardless of the initiating event, the first legal step in the revocation process – the issuance of a *Notice of Intent to Revoke* by CRA to the charity – is always the same. Revocation begins with this notice whether the charity requested the revocation or whether it was initiated by audit. Once the *Notice of Intent to Revoke* (NIR) is issued, legal steps (detailed below) begin and there is a defined process which leads to the finalization of the deregistration of the charity.

As the name implies, the NIR is not the revocation itself, but rather a sign that the CRA intends to proceed to that end. Once the NIR is issued it will only be rescinded if an appeal through the proper process is successful. Despite the importance of the NIR it can be easy to miss as it is simply a letter (rather than a form) where the "re" line states the purpose of the letter.

Actual revocation is only effected with a publication in the *Canada Gazette;* a federal publication that is used to proclaim the legal effectiveness of certain government acts. The Gazette is the official newspaper of the Canadian government, but hardly anyone outside of government reads it.

Each NIR is dated with the date of mailing. This date is important as it is the first day in several timelines. The first is the "winding up" period, the second is the "objection" period, and the third is the date on which the CRA can finalize the revocation with a publication of the notice in the *Canada Gazette*.

Charities can also lose their receipting privileges either temporarily or permanently through suspension or annulment of their privileges by the CRA. In theory, a charity whose receipting privileges are suspended is not in any stage of dissolution, so suspension is not relevant to the present discussion. Annulment, however, can be considered a form of dissolution in that the charity has lost its registered charity status and so it is addressed as well.

VOLUNTARY REVOCATION

Some charities are lucky enough to accomplish the objective that they set out to do and so the need for the charity may evaporate. Other charities run into difficulties raising the necessary funds to continue effective operation and therefore shut down due to business considerations. Still others may suffer from a lack of volunteers. In all of these cases, the board of directors may make the decision that the time has come to shut down the charity and where the charity was registered with the CRA, part of the process will involve a voluntary revocation of the charity.

Under most registration systems, if the registrant no longer wishes to be registered they simply remove themselves from the system. The charity registration system is different in that once registered, the CRA retains the sole ability to remove a charity from the list. "Voluntary" revocation refers to the charity's request of the CRA to exercise its authority to deregister the charity.

Revocation can be requested by writing to:

Charities Directorate
Canada Revenue Agency
Ottawa ON
K1A 0L5

The letter to the CRA need not be any particular format but must be signed by an authorized representative of the charity (as defined by the charity's governing documents). Once received, the CRA will send along the *Notice of Intent to Revoke* which begins the winding up period.

The charity can expect to receive a confirmation that the process of voluntary deregistration has begun and an official *Notice of Intention to Revoke a Charity's Registration* by registered mail. The organization will then have to follow the same procedures regarding the payment of the revocation tax.

FAILURE TO FILE

Technically, revocation for a failure to file is treated similarly to any other type of charitable revocation. Practically speaking, however, this type of revocation is so common that it occupies a special place on the spectrum of reasons for dissolution.

Every registered charity is required to file a yearly information return with the CRA within six months of the end of its fiscal year. Failure to do so is punishable by either a $500 fine or revocation. As a matter of course, charities that fail to file the information return on time receive a reminder notice from the Directorate warning that the charity is in default of filing. If the charity continues in its failure to file, it will receive a *Notice of Intention to Revoke*. However, unlike other causes for revocation, this one has a statutory remedy. A revoked charity can avoid the revocation tax by paying all amounts owing under the either the *Income Tax Act*[9] or the *Excise Tax Act* (although generally there are none in either) and filing all necessary returns under the *Income Tax Act*.

While this may stop the revocation tax from applying, the charity still needs to be re-registered. To do this, the CRA requires the revoked charity to file a *New Application for Registered Charity Status* (form T2050). This new application will be considered like any other new application for registration. Thus the charity bears the risk of being denied registration even though it may have previously been operating as a registered charity, perhaps even for many years. The CRA also applies the controversial practice of requiring the charity to pay an additional $500 for the registration, ostensibly the penalty for missing the filing in the first place.

Technically speaking, a charity could file a *Notice of Objection to an NIR* for failure to file a return but it would be a rare circumstance indeed where a charity could have the revocation withdrawn on such grounds. As such, these types of revocations generally proceed with a re-registration.

REVOCATION FOR CAUSE

The CRA retains the right to revoke a charity's registration for even the slightest infraction of the rules which pertain specifically to charities. (It should be noted that the CRA sometimes tries to argue that a charity should be revoked for infractions for which revocation is not the penalty – such as improper T4s or unpaid source deductions.) However, the CRA has its own set of guidelines which it uses to determine when revocation may be the appropriate remedy.

9 While it is true that charities are known as tax exempt entities they are only exempt under Part I of the Income Tax Act (which is in fact the largest and most important Part), but it is possible that a charity could be taxable under another part of the Income Tax Act.

Generally speaking, revocation is reserved for the most serious cases of non-compliance. This subjective judgment is made by the CRA at its sole discretion – although CRA officers are open to discussion before pursuing this course of action.

There are two ways to avoid revocation for cause. The first is to examine the underlying activity and determine whether, factually, the activity in fact transgressed the law. The second is to argue that revocation is an inappropriate remedy based on the CRA's own guidelines. Generally, the first of these methods is argued most effectively by lawyers trained specifically in the area, while the second area may involve appealing to the CRA officer's own sense of a fair result in the circumstances.

Many charities attempt to argue that revocation is inappropriate because the charity does good work. That approach rarely works. By definition, all registered charities have achieved that status because of the good work they do and the rules apply to all charities equally.

The CRA's guidelines have been previously been published and are available on **www.runningacharity.ca**.

PUBLICATION IN THE GAZETTE

As noted earlier, deregistration is not final until the CRA publishes notice of the revocation in the *Canada Gazette*. Technically, the CRA can publish the notice upon the expiry of 30 days from the date of the NIR but they generally refrain from doing so until the charity has had a chance to exercise its rights of appeal to the Charities Redress Section or the courts. This delay can be very useful in planning what can be done to ensure that those the charities help are not left in the lurch should the charity lose its appeal.

There is no legislated wording for the notice but the notices are simple statements that the CRA revokes the charitable registration of the organization, listing its formal legal name and business number.

The Gazette comes out every Friday at 2 pm in both electronic and print versions. Both are equally definitive. While anyone can subscribe to the Gazette, it is generally only distributed to courts, law libraries and subscribers.

IMMEDIATE REVOCATION

Under certain circumstances the CRA will not hold itself to a delay in finalizing the revocation and will proceed with publication in the Gazette as soon as possible after 30 days from the NIR. The CRA's policy is that it will only pursue this course of action when the charity is engaged in "serious non compliance."

The potential for abuse by the CRA of this policy is clear in that a revoked charity is forced to divest itself of its assets and cannot issue receipts to raise funds to pay for its appeal. At first, the CRA limited itself to immediate revocation only against charities that were involved in tax shelters (an area that the CRA worked for a long time to shut down). But recently, the CRA has begun to look for immediate revocation against other charities including a church and a private school (weeks before the start of the school year).

Immediate revocation of a charity's registration can be fought at the Federal Court of Appeal. There is a three-part test which the Court applies to determine whether it should require the CRA to delay publication. The test looks at the seriousness of the issues involved, whether the harm from a revocation would be irreparable and the balance of convenience. Notably, the test applied by the Court in determining whether or not immediate revocation should proceed is different than the CRA's test as to whether or not it is warranted.

While only one appeal of this type has ever been successful, that one success provided some nuance to the law which may help future charities. Obviously, if a charity wishes to fight an immediate revocation it should seek representation by an experienced lawyer.

WHAT IS THE TAX STATUS OF A REVOKED CHARITY?

Revocation obviously leads to the result that the organization in question is no longer a registered charity, but from a tax perspective if it is not a registered charity then what is it? Clearly, only registered charities can issue charitable donation tax receipts, but the other major question is whether the organization is now taxable on any income it receives as a result of activities or investments.

The answer depends on the nature of the newly revoked organization and the reasons for revocation. The *Income Tax Act* allows for two possibilities; either the organization is now a not- for-profit, and therefore non taxable, or it is a for-profit organization and it must pay tax on its income.

A not-for-profit organization is:

> *"... a club, society or association that, in the opinion of the Minister, was not a charity within the meaning assigned by subsection 149.1(1) and that was organized and operated exclusively for social welfare, civic improvement, pleasure or recreation or for any other purpose except profit, no part of the income of which was payable to, or was otherwise available for the personal benefit of, any proprietor, member or shareholder thereof unless the proprietor, member or shareholder was a club, society or association the primary purpose and function of which was the promotion of amateur athletics in Canada."*[10]

10 Paragraph 149(1)(l) of the Income Tax Act

Interestingly, just because a charity is deregistered does not necessarily imply that the CRA no longer believes the organization is a charity at law – just that it ceases to qualify for status. This is most clearly true in the case of revocation for failure to file. So it cannot be taken as a given that a revoked charity is a not-for-profit. Assuming that, in the Minister's opinion, the organization is still a charity, it would not qualify as a not-for-profit and the income of the charity could become taxable.

The categorization as a charity or a not-for-profit is especially germane when the organization is carrying on a for-profit activity. Charities may conduct business with a view to a profit, not for profits cannot. So if a charity is revoked for some reason, (for example the CRA does not believe it really is a charity at law) it cannot necessarily assume that it can still conduct its business activities in a non-taxable manner.

Any revoked charity that seeks to avoid paying tax on its income should consult a lawyer to determine their technical status.

ANNULMENT

Under certain circumstances, the CRA may annul the charitable registration of any charity. This procedure is only available where the CRA believes it originally registered the charity in error, or the law has changed and if the organization were to apply today it would not qualify for status.

Valid receipts issued prior to the annulment remain as valid receipts. Moreover, the newly annulled charity is not subject to the revocation tax. While it seems that the CRA believes that agreement by the charity is necessary in order to annul the charity's registration this is not the case, and a charity may receive a Notice of Annulment from the CRA to which it may engage in the objection procedure (described earlier in this book).

PROPERTY IN THE CHARITABLE SPHERE

As a matter of policy, the Act is designed so that once property is donated to a registered Canadian charity it will stay within the charitable sector. For example, the Act allows the transfer of receipted property from the recipient charity to another "qualified donee" as that term is defined in the *Income Tax Act*. Consistent with this philosophy, the Act allows for the payment of the so-called "revocation tax" to certain "eligible donees" other than the tax man.

REVOCATION TAX

If the CRA issues a *Notice of Intent to Revoke*, the charity becomes liable to pay a tax effectively equal to the fair market value of its assets on the date of the *Notice of Intention to Revoke* less its debts. The CRA summarizes the calculation as follows:

- The revocation tax is the total value of all remaining assets after all debts and liabilities have been paid. Specifically, it is the total of the following calculation:
    - the fair market value of the charity's property on Day 1;
    - any appropriations that occurred in the 120 day period ending on Day 1; and
    - the income received during the winding-up period.

    Less

    - any expenditures (including amounts spent on charitable activities) during the winding-up period;
    - any debts the charity owes on Day 1; and
    - any property transferred to an eligible donee during the winding-up period.
- **Day 1** is the day after the *Notice of Intent to Revoke* and the winding up period is:
    - the day on which the charity files Form T2046, *Tax Return Where Registration of a Charity is Revoked*, but no later than the day on which the charity is required to file that return;
    - the day on which the Minister last issues a notice of assessment of revocation tax payable under the Act for that taxation year by the charity; and
    - if the charity has filed a *Notice of Objection* or appeal in respect of that assessment, the day on which the Minister may take a collection action under the Act in respect of the tax payable.

Even after the charity's revocation is confirmed, the resolution of an objection to an assessment of revocation tax could itself take several years. The major reason a charity would consider filing a *Notice of Objection* in such circumstances would be a dispute over the value of the charity's assets where the CRA believes more is owing and attempting to extract payment of this alleged excess.

THE WINDING-UP PERIOD

The first time period in which the organization must calculate its revocation tax ends on the date the (now revoked) charity received the *Notice of Intent to Revoke*. The second time period is defined by the Act as the winding-up period of the charity. This period begins on the day *after* the *Notice of Intent to Revoke*, and ends on the latest of three possible dates:

- The day on which the charity files the appropriate returns as described below;
- The day on which the Minister issues a *Notice of Assessment* for the revocation tax; or
- If the charity has filed a notice of objection or appeal in respect of that assessment, the day on which the Minister may take a collection action.

It should be noted that while the winding-up period does not technically include the time period during which the charity objects to and/or appeals the *Notice of Intent to Revoke*, practically speaking the CRA will not issue a notice of assessment of tax until it is determined with certainty that the charity's registration is actually revoked. In fact, the CRA's *RC4424 Guide to Completing the T2046* states explicitly that where a charity objects to the original *Notice of Intent to Revoke*, the CRA will extend the "revocation period" (presumably they mean the winding-up period) to three months *after* all rights of appeal have been exhausted.

During this winding-up period, the charity maintains its receipting privileges and may or may not be a not-for-profit entity. Nevertheless, any income earned by the organization during the winding-up period (including gifts) becomes eligible for the revocation tax. Additionally, certain non-arm's length individuals who receive assets of the charity for less than their fair market value during the winding-up period become liable for the payment of the revocation tax.

A revoked charity may deduct from the assets eligible for the revocation tax anything it spent on charitable activities during the winding-up period. Of course, given that a charity may have its registration revoked due to the CRA disagreeing that its charitable activities are in fact charitable, it can be difficult to make spending decisions and this in itself can lead to a new avenue of dispute.

ELIGIBLE DONEES

As previously outlined, a charity can deduct from the revocation tax payable to the government any payments made to an "eligible donee" during the winding-up period. From a policy perspective, this is consistent with the overall scheme to keep charitable assets in the sector rather than paid to the government. Of course, there is the added benefit that the federal government does not want to be seen seizing the assets of orphanages and schools.

There is a difference between an eligible donee and a qualified donee.

An eligible donee:

- Has 50% or more of its directors dealing at arm's length with the directors of the revoked charity;
- Does not have its registered charity status suspended;
- Has filed all information returns required by the *Income Tax Act*; and
- Is not the subject of a certificate issued under the *Charities Registration (Security Information) Act* or, if it is, the certificate has been determined not to be reasonable.

By comparison, a qualified donee includes:

- Registered charities;
- RCAAAs;
- Certain housing corporations;
- Municipal or public bodies forming a function of government in Canada;
- The United Nations or any of its agencies;
- Certain prescribed universities outside of Canada;
- Certain organizations outside of Canada that have received gifts from the Canadian government; and
- The Crown in right of Canada or a province.

RETURNS UNDER THE INCOME TAX ACT

A revoked charity must file with the Minister a form T2046 – *Tax Return Where Registration of a Charity is Revoked* and the usual T3010A. If the revoked charity fails to file a T2046, the CRA will issue a notice of assessment for revocation tax based on the latest numbers available to the CRA either from the last filed T3010 or audit. It is worthwhile to note that the revoked charity owes this amount as soon as the notice of assessment is issued.

The T2046 form is a technical document, and it could lead to a dispute over revocation tax. It is best filled out by an accountant or other professional individual with knowledge of the organization's finances.

NOTICES OF OBJECTION

If the charity disagrees with the amount of the assessment, it may file a *Notice of Objection* within 90 days of the date on the *Notice of Assessment*. The usual circumstance in which a revoked charity might do this is when the CRA has assessed the wrong amount. If the CRA is unaware of the more recent financial circumstances of the charity, such that the value of the assets has declined since the latest T3010, or were disbursed in the course of charitable activities, or were transferred to an appropriate party, the assessment will be incorrect. Consequently, the revoked charity will either have to file a *Notice of Objection* or pay an assessment for funds it no longer has.

While a *Notice of Objection* for a private taxpayer is sent to the Chief of Appeals at the various Tax Services Offices, it should be noted that a *Notice of Objection* to either a *Notice of Intent to Revoke* or a *Notice of Assessment* against a charity is sent to the:

> **Assistant Commissioner**
> Appeals Branch
> 250 Albert Street, 13th Floor
> Ottawa ON
> K1A 0L5

It is important to note that unless the charity is not incorporated, or the directors have misappropriated the charity's assets, the assessment for tax will only be against the organization and not the individuals running the charity.

OTHER IMPLICATIONS OF REVOCATION

With the possible exception of charities whose registration is annulled because of a change to the law, the fact that a charity is no longer registered with the CRA does not necessarily mean that the common law applying to charities no longer applies to it. In particular, the fiduciary duties that attach to specified gifts must be kept in mind when disbursing all of a charity's assets. At all times, the terms of the specified gifts should be adhered to (whether by a new charity or an eligible donee that accepts upon itself those obligations). If the terms can no longer be met, the organization may have to apply to the court under the *Cy-Près* doctrine for guidance.

APPENDIX A - CURRENT MODEL OBJECTS

Relief of poverty

To relieve poverty by operating a food bank for [specify eligible beneficiaries, for example, individuals or families who are poor, of low income, or in need].

To relieve poverty by operating a soup kitchen for [specify eligible beneficiaries, for example, individuals or families who are poor, of low income, or in need].

To relieve poverty by providing basic necessities of life, including food, clean water, clothing, and/or shelter to [specify eligible beneficiaries, for example, individuals or families who are poor, of low income, or in need].

To relieve poverty by providing food and other basic necessities of life to [specify eligible beneficiaries, for example, individuals or families who are poor, of low income, or in need].

To relieve poverty by establishing, operating and maintaining shelters for the homeless.

To relieve poverty by providing residential accommodation below market rate, support, and incidental facilities to [specify eligible beneficiaries, for example, individuals or families who are poor, of low income, or in need].

Relief of poverty – Developing nations

To relieve poverty in developing nations by providing food and other basic necessities of life to individuals or families in need.

To relieve poverty in developing nations by providing basic necessities of life, including food, clean water, clothing, and/or shelter to [specify eligible beneficiaries, for example, individuals or families who are poor, of low income, or in need].

Relief of poverty – Disaster relief

To relieve poverty by providing necessities of life, including food, clean water, medical supplies, clothing, and/or shelter to victims of disasters.

Advancement of education

To advance education by establishing and operating a public [primary, secondary, or post-secondary] school for [specify eligible beneficiaries] [if required, specify topic(s)].

To advance education by providing books, equipment, and educational aids to students attending [specify name of school].

To advance education by providing classes on the subjects of childbirth education, preparation for parenting, and nutrition to [specify].

To advance education by providing leadership training programs to [specify eligible beneficiary group].

To advance education by providing publicly available scholarships, bursaries, and other forms of financial assistance to [specify eligible beneficiaries] to be used for [specify, elementary, secondary, or postsecondary] education.

To advance education by providing awards to [specify eligible beneficiaries] to encourage academic excellence.

To advance education by training police officers, teachers, social workers, and crisis response workers to recognize and respond to online sexual exploitation and to assist children and youth affected by this issue.

To advance education by operating a science fair for students across Canada.

Advancement of education – Arts

To advance education by providing instructional seminars on topics related to the performing and visual arts to [specify eligible beneficiaries].

Advancement of religion

To advance religion by teaching the religious tenets, doctrines, and observances associated with [specify religion or faith].

To advance religion by preaching the teachings, and religious tenets, doctrines and observances, associated with [specify faith or religion].

To advance religion by establishing and maintaining a house of worship with services conducted (or held) in accordance with the tenets and doctrines of [specify faith or religion].

To advance religion by establishing and maintaining a religious school of instruction on the subject of [specify faith or religion] for [specify children, youths, and/or adults].

To advance religion by establishing a facility to be used for religious programs, workshops, music, and [specify for example Bible, Qur'anic, Talmudic or other] studies.

Other purposes that are beneficial to the community in a way the law considers charitable.

Promotion of health

To promote health by providing the public with [specify type of] medical services.

To promote health by providing affected populations with health care services or products that prevent and manage serious threats to health and survival.

To promote health by providing accident victims with physical, occupational, or speech therapy.

To promote health by protecting and maintaining public health through the operation of a healthy-heart program to slow the development and progression of heart disease.

To promote health by providing individuals with [specify health condition] with access to related counselling, information, or group support programs.

To promote health by providing public ambulance, paramedic, or firefighting services.

Advancing the public's appreciation of the arts

To advance the public's appreciation of the arts by providing high-quality artistic performances in [specify for example, public places, senior citizens homes, churches, community centres, and educational institutions].

To advance the public's appreciation of the arts by producing public art exhibitions, presentations, and performance art(s) events, and by providing a forum for qualified artists to exhibit, present, or perform their artistic works through participation in such events.

To advance the public's appreciation of the arts by:
- providing high-quality public performances of classical choral works; and
- providing free performances for audiences that may not be able to attend regular performances.

Protection of the environment

Ecosystem preservation.

To protect the environment for the benefit of the public by conserving or restoring ecosystems and biodiversity on a long-term basis.

Pollution reduction

To protect the environment for the benefit of the public by conserving ecosystems through saving, supporting, protecting, or assisting stressed or endangered forms of life (including plant and animal life).

To protect the environment for the benefit of the public by reducing pollution for the benefit of the public by operating a water testing and treatment program at [specify location].

To protect the environment for the benefit of the public by reducing pollution and by cleaning up or remediating polluted [specify air, water, or ground].

Promoting the welfare of animals

To promote the welfare of animals for the benefit of the public by spaying or neutering domestic pets, and/or feral or stray animals.

To promote the welfare of animals for the benefit of the public by:
- rescuing stray, abandoned, abused, or surrendered animals; and
- operating an animal adoption program.

Addressing and preventing specific problems faced by children or youth

To address and prevent problems faced by children or youth by providing publicly available crisis counselling.

To address and prevent problems faced by children by operating a latchkey program for [specify eligible beneficiaries, for example, children attending public elementary schools].

To address and prevent problems faced by youth by operating a supervised youth centre (or drop-in centre) that provides structured programs directed toward resolving [specify the problem(s)].

To address and prevent problems faced by youth by establishing, operating, and maintaining a long-term group home for youth dealing with [specify problem(s)].

To address and prevent problems faced by youth by establishing, operating, and maintaining a life-skills learning centre for Aboriginal children and youth dealing with [specify problem(s)].

Addressing and preventing specific problems faced by families

To address and prevent specific problems faced by families by establishing and operating an assessment and counselling center for children, youth, and parents dealing with behaviour management issues.

To address and prevent specific problems faced by families by providing parents, children, and youth with mentoring programs, workshops, and seminars on issues such as anger management, conflict resolution, and effective communication.

To address and prevent specific problems faced by families by providing grief support and counselling for survivors that addresses issues associated with the loss of family members.

To address and prevent specific problems faced by families by providing counselling and outreach programs to individuals affected by family violence.

Relieving conditions associated with the aged.

To relieve conditions associated with the aged by providing specially adapted residential accommodation, incidental facilities, and support to [specify eligible beneficiaries].

To relieve conditions associated with the aged by providing personal care, housekeeping, meals, nursing, shopping assistance, and transportation to medical appointments to [specify eligible beneficiaries].

Relieving conditions associated with disability

To relieve conditions associated with disability by providing specially adapted residential accommodation, incidental facilities, and support to [specify eligible beneficiaries].

To relieve conditions associated with disability by providing trained personnel and specialized services that assist [specify eligible beneficiaries] in their daily activities.

To relieve conditions associated with disability by providing athletic and recreational programs to support the physical, mental, and emotional well-being of [specify eligible beneficiaries].

To relieve conditions associated with disability by providing life management counselling and other supportive services to [specify eligible beneficiaries] to become and remain more independent in the community.

To relieve conditions associated with disability by providing job training and job placement assistance to [specify eligible beneficiaries].

To relieve conditions associated with disability by providing camps with specially adapted programs and facilities for children or youth with [specify condition(s)].

To relieve conditions associated with disability by providing assistive devices to [specify eligible beneficiaries].

Providing public amenities

To provide a public amenity by establishing and maintaining a memorial garden for the public.

To provide a public amenity by establishing and maintaining a park in [specify community].

To provide a public amenity by establishing and maintaining a public children's playground].

To provide a public amenity by establishing, administering, and maintaining a multi-use recreational facility in [specify community].

To provide a public amenity by establishing and maintaining a [specify type of museum] for the public.

Protecting and preserving significant heritage sites.

To protect and preserve significant heritage sites by restoring, developing, and maintaining the [specify the historic site] with a view to commemorating the site and educating the public about it.

Promoting the efficiency of the Canadian Armed Forces.

To promote the efficiency of the Canadian Armed Forces for the benefit of the public by providing [air, sea, or army] cadet training to youth.

Promoting commerce or industry

To promote and maintain efficiency and high standards of practice in the [specify industry, trade, or profession] for the benefit of the public by developing training programs for, and providing funds for the training of, individuals engaged in the [industry, trade or profession].

To promote excellence and efficiencies in the [specify industry, trade or profession] in Canada for the benefit of the public by establishing and maintaining best practices and standards of workmanship, through the development and institution of an apprenticeship program.

To promote excellence in the [specify industry, trade or profession] in Canada for the benefit of the public by conducting research on best practices related to that [specify industry, trade or profession] and disseminating the results of the research to the public.

Gifting to qualified donees

Ontario -

To receive and maintain a fund or funds and to apply all or part of the principal and income therefrom, from time to time, to charitable organizations that are also registered charities under the *Income Tax Act* (Canada).

For all other Canadian jurisdictions -

To receive and maintain a fund or funds and to apply all or part of the principal and income there from, from time to time, to qualified donees as defined in subsection 149.1(1) of the *Income Tax Act* (Canada).

INDEX

I

J

L

M

N

O

P

Q

R

S